PARENTING

DaRn
GOOd
AdVicE
PARENTING

Jan Faull, M.Ed. Illustrated by David Hitch

To my children Anna, Jerry, and Alan.

First edition for the United States, its territories and dependencies, and Canada published in 2006 by Barron's Educational Series, Inc.

Design: **Balley Design Associates**

All inquiries should be addressed to:
Barron's Educational Series, Inc.
250 Wireless Boulevard
Hauppauge, NY 11788
www.barronseduc.com

ISBN-13: 978-0-7641-3226-1
ISBN-10: 0-7641-3226-1

Library of Congress Control Number: 2005920909

Printed in Italy
9 8 7 6 5 4 3 2 1

Contents

PrEfAcE

Did you ever think that in one day you would be wallowing in self-pity because you can't make a phone call without interruptions and feeling overwhelmed with love and pride because your child wrote her name for the first time?

You probably never thought of yourself as a referee, but there you are watching your children battle it out while you decide whether to stop it, watch it, or walk away. Episodes take place minute-by-minute in parenting, some of which you can handle with ease, others of which leave you outraged or tongue-tied.

Parents need advice and darn good advice at that. There's lots of it in the pages to follow. Read it. But before you use it, mull it over in your head. Ask yourself, "Does this piece of advice apply to me and my children?" If it does, try out the approach to see if it fits with your style of parenting and the personality of your child. Adjust it until it begins to feel a natural part of your parenting repertoire.

Be a good consumer of parenting information. Use what you can to help you become the best parent you can be, file some of it away for a later date, pass some of it on to other parents, and discard some while saying, "This may make sense to other parents but not to me."

The advice contained in the pages to come has one main purpose in mind: for you to parent in the best interest of your children's emotional and mental health and well being. It's also provided so that you can secure a loving and liking relationship with your children. The goal for readers is to learn to move quickly through the rough spots in parenting with grace so that you can enjoy your children as you support and encourage them to reach their potential.

If nothing else, take time each day to observe your children as they learn to tie their shoes, play imaginatively in the backyard, or complete a homework assignment. By doing so you'll gain insights and appreciation into this amazing person growing up right before your eyes. By observing, you'll be a more satisfied parent with fewer regrets as each child leaves home, and you'll know you've done your job right.

About the author

Jan Faull, M.Ed., has taught Parent Education for more than twenty-five years, she is a recognized speaker to a wide variety of parenting organizations, and she developed a training program along with a team from the Comprehensive Health Education Foundation titled Social Beginnings: Guiding Children Toward Positive Behavior.

Jan writes a weekly column for *The Seattle Times*, is the Parent Advisor for *Ladies Home Journal* and *Better Homes & Gardens'* online services, the Family Consultant to Disney's online service for parents, Family.com, and the Parenting Expert to the morning show, Seattle Live.

She is the author of two books, *Mommy, I have to Go Potty* and *Unplugging Parent-Child Power Struggles: Resolving Emotional Battles with Your Kids Ages 2–10.*

Jan is a mother of three and grandmother of one. She resides in her empty nest in Seattle, Washington.

Throughout this book, when referring to the infant or child, I have tried to alternate the use of "he" and "she" by chapter. This has been done to avoid the impersonal "it" or the sometimes awkward use of the plural form. No gender bias is intended by this writing style.

CHAPTER 1
NURTURING THE FAMILY

ArE yOu A NuRtUrInG pArEnT?

You're a parent. You're the mother or father of your children.
You are the very source that produced them, the one who
brought them into your home. But you are so much more.
You are the person who feeds and protects your children, who
supports and encourages their development. You are bringing up
your children by guiding, training, and educating them. This job
description defines you as a nurturer.

It's unlikely that you walk around wearing a pin that declares, "I'm a
nurturer." You most likely use other terms to describe yourself.
Perhaps "strict disciplinarian." Or possibly you see yourself as a 1960s
hippie: laid back and encouraging your children to do their own thing.
You may feel yourself flitting from one parenting situation to the next,
putting out familial fires, tending to one mini-crisis or conflict after
another, offering comfort and reassurance.

Which parenting personality are you?
❑ Are you a pushy parent or a pushover?
❑ Do you seamlessly morph from coach to guide to teacher?
❑ Would friends and family call you touchy-feely or distant?
❑ Are you over- or under-protective?
❑ Do you go by the book or shoot from the hip?

Answer: Most parents play most of these roles at different times
in their parenting lives. The key to success and satisfaction is to
know which part to play in the parenting scenario at hand.

Ultimate nurturing

You'll fare better in the big picture of your parenting life if, rather than seeing yourself merely as the person who brings a child into the home and keeps her there about eighteen years, you view yourself as the one responsible for nurturing her development.

Nurturing parents adjust their role depending on the child's developmental age. It's asking a lot, but if you can bear to wear the many different parenting hats your role offers and sometimes demands, you'll have a much easier time of it. Nurturing parents know you don't parent both toddlers and teens with the same considerations or expectations. The nurturing parent knows when to indulge the child with love and attention, and when to say "no" and mean it.

Are you a nurturing parent? Review the checklist on the next page to determine which attributes of the nurturing parent describe you. Many of them probably come naturally, so pat yourself on the back and give yourself credit. If you find a couple of weak spots, it's not too late to incorporate them into your parenting repertoire.

ThE nUrTuRiNg PaReNt'S cHeCkLiSt

1 Are you always affectionate and friendly when interacting with your children? The nurturing parent expresses affection and friendliness by . . .

❑ Saying "I love you" with words and a gentle touch. You love your children so why not say it—and show it? Each time you lovingly touch a child, you're communicating love without saying a word.

❑ Expressing love and limits at the same time. This means that when you say, "No, I won't allow you to do that," you add, "It's only because I'm concerned about your well-being, because I love you so much."

❑ Spending time with each child in mutually enjoyable activities that particularly interest her. When you read a story or play with blocks on your child's terms, you're offering her the most precious commodity you have—your time and attention.

2 Don't you just hate parents who gush? When speaking to your child, don't go overboard with statements like, "You're so great!" or "You're absolutely fabulous!" A more subtle approach means more to a child as she masters the skills expected in childhood.
The nurturing parent . . .

❑ Notices small steps to competency. The first time your child awkwardly scribbles her name, you know to post it on the refrigerator. You don't wait for perfection.

❑ Says, "I like it when . . ." and "I appreciate it when . . ." When children live up to your expectations, when they comply, let them know you appreciate it. "I really appreciate that you carried your plate from the table to the counter."

❑ Watches out for criticism. It's your job to teach your child many tasks, but make sure your critical comments don't take the wind out of a child's learning sails. If your child just learned how to button but missed one on her sweater, don't point it out right away. Don't be a perfectionist. Another day, show her how to carefully match up the buttons and buttonholes.

❑ Describes and observes a child's accomplishments. As a child is attempting a task, give a play-by-play account or just watch. Your quiet comments and mere presence will encourage your children's positive actions. All it takes is "Well done, you learned to ride your bike! Show me how you do it. I want to watch."

3 Do you consider your children's feelings, needs, and desires? Consideration does not mean indulging children, giving in to their every whim, or spoiling them. It means considering their wants while keeping their best interests in mind. The nurturing parent does so by ...

❏ Asking a child her opinion. All it takes is a simple question, such as, "What would you like for dinner?" or "What park would you like to go and play at today?"

❏ Reiterating and respecting the child's point of view. When a child says "I would really like my bed next to this wall," you could respond with, "You want to move your bed? Let me think about it."

❏ Affirming their ideas and going along with them when appropriate, possible, and reasonable. "I know you really want a puppy, but I don't think we can get one this year. Maybe when you're ten years old, and we can work on what's involved in caring for a puppy."

❏ Encouraging the expression of negative feelings, but not permitting any accompanying negative behavior. "I know that you're jealous of the baby. I understand that. I'm glad you told me. But I can't allow you to poke her because you may hurt her."

4 Are you interested in your child's daily activities? Of course you are. The nurturing parent proves it by . . .

❏ Completing the cycle of the conversation. When your child announces, "My team won at recess today," respond with an interested inquiry: "What was the score?" This tells your child that you've heard what she said, that you're interested, and that you want to hear more.

❏ Going to her events and supporting her activities and interests. You not only go to soccer practices and games but you cheer your child on even if she never kicks a goal or, for that matter, the ball!

❏ Noticing when a child comes and goes. Children need to know that their presence or absence makes a difference to you. A simple, "Hi, I'm glad you're home," or "You're going out to play? What time will you be back?" is all it takes.

5 Do you offer support and encouragement during times of stress?
The nurturing parent . . .

❏ Offers empathy and understanding when a child is upset, for
example, "Yes, it is so sad that our kitty died."

❏ Expresses faith that things will eventually get better. "I know you feel
so sad today about the cat dying. You will always remember her but you
won't always feel as sad as you do right now."

❏ Encourages and is available for the child to discuss the stressful
situation. "When you want to talk about your kitty, just let me know. We
can even write a story about her life."

❏ Encourages the child to come up with ideas to solve the problem.
"What can you do so you won't feel so sad? Do you want a picture of
kitty by your bed? Let's find one and put it in a frame."

How do you measure up? If you're nurturing 60 percent of the time,
you're doing a darn good job. Keep it up! The antithesis of nurturing is
being unnecessarily controlling, harsh, distant, or punishing. If you work
on your nurturing skills—they'll pay back long-term benefits to you
and your children.

The benefits of being a nurturing parent:
- You put your children on the road to good mental health.
- Your children will naturally work to reach their potential.
- When you flub up in the parenting arena, the fallout is temporary; your relationship with your child bounces back quickly.
- Your children remain open to your influence.
- You deter the negative influences of popular culture.
- You serve as a buffer to unsavory forms of peer pressure.
- Your children feel cared for and loved.

MoThers, nUrTuRe YoUr SeLf-EsTeEm

Think back to when you brought your first baby into the world. What feelings and memories come to mind? Were you fulfilled, competent, and in control? Or did you feel disorganized and awkward, questioning why you ever entered the world of motherhood?

Most new moms experience a mix of emotions. But it's likely that you stood in awe at the human being you created and felt overwhelmed with love, devotion, and responsibility.

Many women step joyously into their parenting role and the responsibilities come naturally. Others are shaken by fatigue, repetition, and the realization that they've embarked on a demanding 24/7 job with no paychecks or promotions.

Sometimes parenting seems to be a no-win guilt trip. If you're a stay-at-home mom, people keep asking what you do all day. If you work outside the home, they ask, "How can you bear to drop your kids at child care?" If you're a single mom going it alone, your life as the primary caregiver may become overwhelming and burdensome.

Don't buy into the traditional thinking that moms have a "parenting gene" in their DNA and that childrearing just comes naturally. When your child exhibits behavior problems, difficulties with learning, or a handicapping condition, your self-image and self-esteem are bound to suffer.

Hey! How do *you* feel?

Do you feel trapped? Do your days overflow with giving, nurturing—and setting your own needs aside for your children? If so, don't be surprised if your self-esteem plummets. When it does, you'll probably resort to yelling, spanking, crying, complaining, overeating, clamming up, or just plain giving up. This behavior doesn't make for pleasant and productive days. Moreover, when you've completely blown it and labeled the day an absolute disaster, you'll have to pull yourself together to face it all again tomorrow.

For the short run, try taking a warm bath, going for a walk, calling a friend, buying yourself a special treat, praying, taking a nap, reading, or cranking up the music and dancing to rock 'n' roll with the kids. You must take care of yourself or you won't be able to continue to give your all to your children.

For the long run, think of what you can do on a regular basis to prevent burning out from the demands of parenting. Most moms start out with few skills, little knowledge, and zero experience. Attending a parenting class or reading books about raising kids can help. Getting together with other moms to compare notes, information, and horror stories can be equally satisfying.

Make time for me-time

Some moms seek out hobbies or activities completely separate from parenting, such as reading a novel, taking a course, or joining an exercise program. A watercolor class, piano lessons, or a gardening club can revive you and boost your foundering self-worth.

Remember that no two moms have the same needs. Some return to work to stay sane, while others quit their jobs or find part-time employment to spend more time at home. You need a break at least once a week from the kids, as well as regular exercise and a schedule that doesn't overextend your energies.

Motherhood offers few tangible rewards, and there's no awards banquet or financial bonus at the end of the day. The bonuses come when your child learns to read, rides a bike, spontaneously helps with the dishes, and automatically says "please" and "thank you."

Look for the little gems that are cherished by you alone. A little boy, Andrew, approaches his mom and says, "Mom, I want to buy you a ring. Will you take me to the store? It's just because you're such a good Mommy." Of course, Mom drives Andrew to the store where he picks out a $1.75 ring. Mom wears it proudly.

Then there's Monti. She worked extra hours while she attended college to send her parents to Hawaii, explaining that she just wanted Mom and Dad to know how much she appreciated all they've done for her over the years.

The Montis of this world are rare. Don't feel you've failed if you don't get a trip to Hawaii. The important reward is in raising responsible, respectful children. If you want to put your children on the path to success, you must first develop and nurture your own motherhood self-esteem.

You've come a long way, Daddy

Today's dad is often right there when baby takes that first breath. He changes diapers, takes kids to the doctor, and hauls the diaper bag, car seat, and toddler off to child care. He even takes vacation time to attend school programs and conferences.

And dad is no longer just the disciplinarian. The old adage, "Wait until your dad gets home," is now passé. Dad doesn't want to be feared; of course he is involved in disciplining the children but he wants to nurture, too.

Checklist for Dad

Some dads have the responsibility of full-time care of a child, either as a stay-at-home dad or as a single parent. For them, the task can be just as overwhelming as it's always been for moms. Here are a few pointers . . .

• Realize that your involvement is not simply to help out Mom because it's fun or the "in" thing to do. You're into parenting because it's your responsibility; children are more secure and are more likely to reach their potential when they know you really care.

• Realize that your sons learn to be men from you. Without you he'll flounder; he'll lean toward peer groups or even gangs. It will be more difficult for him to develop self-control.

• Realize that your daughters learn about relationships with men by having a good relationship first with you. If you ignore her or even reject her, she may fear rejection from all men in future relationships.

• Realize that if you are a dad who was raised in a traditional family where Mom stayed home with the kids and made all the decisions about child rearing and Dad worked to pay the bills, this is the only parenting model that you know.

• Realize that even if you want to be more involved with your children, you may not know how to go about doing so. Maybe you're frustrated because your wife can calm your screaming infant and you can't. Or when you try to put the kids to bed they cry because you don't do Mom's routine. And they always seem to run to her and not you when they're sad or hurt and want comforting.

• Realize that you may just need to jump in and do it. Let trial and error be your teacher. You'll determine your role right along with your kids.

Why the change?

Mom decided she was tired of raising the kids all by herself, so she demanded help. She also wanted or needed to work outside the home, so Dad had to get involved.

And then Dad began to experience the joys of parenting. He enjoyed reading those stories from Dr. Seuss about *The Sneetches* "with stars upon thars"; he was frightened along with the kids in discovering *Where the Wild Things Are*, Maurice Sendak's classic book about the fragile line between fantasy and reality; and he giggled at the antics of *Mrs. Piggle-Wiggle* by Betty MacDonald.

Dad never had Legos when he was growing up, and he found that helping the kids put them together is fun. Sometimes the kids have to watch out as Dad often becomes a Lego maniac.

For some divorced dads it's harder to be involved because the kids live with their mom. But today's non-custodial dad doesn't simply settle for every other weekend, and he's not just a Disneyland dad.

He wants more time, involvement, and influence. He's not only there for the trips to the zoo, he's also involved in putting together the telegraph for the science fair.

Jump in and just do it, you'll figure it out

- Send Mom out one evening a week and take over. Do it your way, and let the kids complain. It's just the change from Mom's way to Dad's way that they don't like—eventually, they'll get comfortable with your style of parenting.
- Find an activity that you and your children enjoy doing together and do it on a regular basis. Take your baby to visit Grandma, take your toddler to the park, your pre-schooler to the hardware store, your school-age child to your workplace, and your teenager to a ball game.
- Hang in there as your children get older. Don't just stick around for the fun times: Be there for the tough times, too. When your children are younger, you'll need to help with homework, step in to settle sibling fights, and help the kids tidy their rooms.
- Stay involved though the thick and thin of parenting. As your children get older, the tough times may get tougher. If your daughter gets caught stealing eye shadow, leave work and come home; your presence at this time is crucial. When your son experiences his first break-up with a girl, don't pooh-pooh his feelings; give him a hug and listen to his heartbreak.
- It's easy to have quality time when things are going well. It's making it through the tough times with dignity that determines a quality dad.

21st Century Dad

In the 1950s, there was a television comedy show called *Make Room for Daddy* in which the dad, played by Danny Thomas, was a bit of a buffoon. In this new century, there's plenty of room for Dad, and he's not just the breadwinner or disciplinarian, he's much more. He's loving, nurturing, involved, interested, and vital to the emotional, social, and intellectual health of his children. He's a pal to his kids and also protector of the family.

ThE hArDeSt JoB oF all— SiNgLe PaReNtInG

Here's advice from three single moms for other parents—moms and dads—going it alone.

Taking time for yourself. There's no way that your children won't be your top priority, but beware of allowing your kids to totally consume you. Get a baby-sitter or ask a friend for a favor and go out for personal time on a regular basis. Arranging free time is more difficult for single parents, but at the same time, it's more important, too. You know you need more adult interaction if at work you're using the word "potty" instead of "bathroom."

Overcompensating. Realize that although you try, you can't really make up for the missing parent. You're probably over-compensating if you find yourself playing princess with your daughter one minute and loving it and then wrestling with her the next but hating it. Stop yourself when you're aware that you're overcompensating for the absentee father.

Broadening relationships. Involve both you and your child in activities where there are adults of the same sex as the absentee parent. These could be members of your religious group, or co-workers and family friends—look to people with whom your child is comfortable. Be around traditional families too. It's a broadening experience for your child to see there are a variety of ways to be a family.

Using the family. Keep in contact with relatives—grandparents, cousins, aunts, and uncles. Your children need to know that they have an extended family who love, show interest in, and support their family.

Asking for help from friends. When you or your child is sick, or when you feel unsafe, you'll need to call out for assistance from the support group of relatives, friends, and neighbors you've cultivated.

A positive output. Do your best to speak positively and tactfully about the other parent but at the same time answer your children's questions. Explain situations regarding the absentee parent matter-of-factly, without impugning motive.

Offering explanations, with love in mind. Avoid discussing child support issues with your children, no matter what their age. Even though you may feel anger, irritation, and abandonment, it's your job and responsibility to set aside your feelings for the children's sake. No editorial comments are allowed, just present the facts, cushioned for the soft little hearts and minds of your children. Even if a father chooses not to be a part of his children's lives it's important for the mother to say, "Deep in your father's heart he loves you. He lives far away so it's difficult for him to visit. If you like, you can draw a picture and we'll mail it to him."

Keeping sensible boundaries. It's important for the custodial parent to not see the child as a buddy. Although you can usually come across as friendly, you're not your child's best friend nor is your son or daughter yours. If you play the role of buddy or girlfriend to your child, when it's time to step in and say "no" you'll be reluctant to do so because you'll fear losing that best friend status.

Stepping out of the zone. Determine the types of family activities such as camping or hiking that you would have done as a couple, and try to do them even though you're on your own. When you stretch yourself to go beyond your comfort zone, you're really providing the upbringing and activities that will benefit your child.

Making friends. Become involved in your child's activities—coaching team sports, participating in PTA, or Sunday school. When you do, your child's friends and their parents will get to know you, and this will help them to feel comfortable with their children spending time in the home of a single parent. Unfortunately, there is still a stigma attached to single parent homes.

Sharing the joys. What's most difficult about being a single parent? There's no one to share the pride or pain. The day your child first walks, rides a bike, learns to read, or even becomes valedictorian, the obvious person—the child's mom or dad—may not be available or willing to chime in with the joys of the child's accomplishments. If your child doesn't follow the teacher's instructions, doesn't complete assignments, dawdles, whines, or pouts, with whom do you share your concern? If your young adult is arrested for underage driving and drinking, who do you seek for comfort?

How do *you* fit in? The person lending a hand or an ear to a parent raising children alone could be a variety of parent substitutes. Could that person possibly be you?

Debbie's single mom story

Debbie, a single mom of three, worried that she wasn't instilling the right values in her children.

On Saturdays the children were either with their dad or she would take them to visit Grandma or to the park, library, or free community events at shopping malls or museums. If her budget allowed, she'd take them to the movies. On Sundays she was busy doing the laundry and grocery shopping, and then she'd cook at least one large casserole or soup that she could heat up for dinner the next week.

During the week she'd gather her kids from school and child care, head home, and serve dinner in the kitchen. The kids would sit in front of the TV to eat as she quickly read the mail. She'd offer a reminder about homework and make sure one or two took a bath before tucking them into bed with a kiss and a hug. Sometimes, but not always, she'd read a bedtime story and talk about their day as she tucked them into bed.

Often, at this late hour, she had no energy, so she would just fall into bed. Sometimes in the middle of the night the youngest would climb in with her.

Then Debbie paused. What could she change about their day to make room for family time and values? She decided that after serving up the kids' plates from the kitchen, she could insist that they sit at the table together and eat. She could, by sitting her children around the table, instill love and interest in each other. She would ask them each about their day with specific questions: "What did you eat for lunch?" "What was the best part of your day and what was the worst?" "Did you do something nice for another person?" "Did someone do something nice for you?"

Although this little alteration in her family's day wasn't drastic, it did make a significant difference in their lives: It was a daily solidification of the family. It's what this single mom could do, and in the long-term life of her family it meant a lot.

PaReNtInG tOgEtHeR

Maintaining a good relationship with your spouse is beneficial for both you and your children. You may think your children constantly want to be the center of attention, but deep in their hearts, when they know their parents have a good relationship, they feel secure. The paramount rule for parenting together is to cultivate and foster your partnership. Go out of your way to show your children that you and your spouse have a relationship beyond them.

Confirm your relationship by . . .
- Going on dates.
- Closing your bedroom door and insisting your children knock.
- Teaching your children not to interrupt your conversations.
- Making sure the kids realize you've made up after an argument.
- Kissing and hugging each other affectionately—not passionately—in front of the kids.

Once you understand the importance of nurturing your relationship, it's time to focus on how you're going to parent together. By parenting together effectively, not only do you preserve your relationship, but you also come across to your children as being respectful to one another.

You and your spouse were raised by different parents. You are different people, so it should come as no surprise that you approach parenting differently. Most parents share similar goals and values for their children; however, the path toward those goals is often a source of conflict. Let's say you both want your children to be polite, but Dad believes setting a good example is all it takes, and Mom takes a more active approach of correcting each slip-up. Both strategies can be effective, but as parents, you may want to find common ground.

THE rulE bOOK fOr PaRENtInG tOgEtHeR

Because you'll frequently be put to the test, make sure you brush up on these guidelines for harmonious parenting when there are two sets of opinions.

Rule No. 1: Don't undermine your partner.
It's too easy to let this happen on a daily basis. Your spouse says to your four-year-old, "You may not ride your tricycle into the street." You disagree, saying, "I think it's OK for Tommy to ride in the cul-de-sac. Go ahead Tommy, it's OK."

This is a parenting-together "no-no." You undermined your spouse, making him appear powerless to your child. It is far better to discuss tricycle rules away from the eyes and ears of your child.
Exception: If your spouse is physically or emotionally abusing your child, you have a right and responsibility to step in to protect your child.

Rule No. 2: The parent who administers the discipline carries it out.
Your preschooler colored on her bedroom walls. You discover the mess, reprimand her, and demand she clean the walls herself. She throws a temper tantrum and refuses to wipe the crayon marks off the wall. Now what?

You're exasperated, plus you're expected at a meeting in 30 minutes, so you call on your spouse to calm her down. "And make sure she cleans the crayon marks off the wall," you say, as you hurry off and leave him to exercise discipline.

Oops! Another "no-no." If you set the discipline, it's up to you to follow through and carry it out.

Rule No. 3: You don't have to always present a united front.
You don't eat ice cream and you would not like your kids to eat it either. Your spouse is an ice cream freak. He occasionally piles the kids into the car for a trip to Dairy Queen.

Let them go. This issue doesn't involve safety or values, and it's okay for each of you to present a separate position.

Rule No. 4: Develop a parent time-out signal.
You know the sign—make a T with your fingers. Agree with your spouse to use this signal when either of you witnesses a parent-child altercation that's going on and on with no resolution in sight. It's easier for you to gain some perspective and resolve the conflict after you've taken a little break.

Rule No. 5: If a child is abusive, ask for backup.
When one parent is clashing with a child, and the child starts hitting, talking back, or arguing relentlessly, it's appropriate to ask for backup from the other parent. Your child will catch on quicker if she's defeated by both parents saying, "No" or "Stop."

Rule No. 6: Avoid heated battles in front of the kids.
It's OK for kids to see Mom and Dad disagree or even argue.
However, heated emotional fights can frighten and worry children. If
your children do witness a nasty argument, make sure that they see
you resolve it and make up.

Rule No. 7: Don't bad-mouth your spouse.
Parenting takes integrity. Even if your spouse was being a bit of a jerk
to you or your kids, hold your tongue. Children love and are loyal to
both parents. If your spouse wrongs the child, don't chime in. Instead,
empathize and try to explain the situation.

Rule No. 8: Respect your partner's parenting style.
Recognize that your style of parenting will be different from your
spouse's. Different approaches help children adjust to differences in
people's personalities. Dad can't be a mom and Mom can't be a dad.
That's why your children need you both.

Rule No. 9: Praise your parenting partner.
Parenting is difficult, exhausting, and time consuming. Take time to show
appreciation for what your spouse does for the kids. No one gets
medals for parenting. Praise and accolades only come to you from
each other.

Rule No. 10: Watch how you offer parenting advice.
Usually one parent reads more parenting information or takes more
parenting classes than the other. Your enthusiasm for a new approach
to discipline may make your spouse feel defensive or insecure. Gently
offer information, but realize that unsolicited advice can often be
taken as criticism.

Final points

When you and your spouse disagree about parenting, make sure your argument is truly about the kids and not really about another unresolved problem in your relationship.

If you are in a parenting power struggle, seek professional help. Emotional power plays only damage your relationship and negatively affect your children.

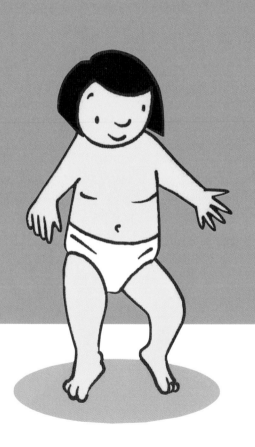

CHAPTER 2
BROTHERS AND SISTERS

ThE nOt So BlEsSeD eVeNt

The time leading up to the birth of your second child brings out a mixed bag of parenting emotions:

- **Excitement** about bringing a new child into the world.
- **Curiosity** as to what this new child will be like.
- **Worry** about caring for and managing two children.
- **Concern** that you will be able to meet not only your children's needs, but your own.

When you emerge from being totally overwhelmed by the production of another little miracle, your thoughts most likely will turn to your firstborn. He clearly will not view the birth of a sibling as a blessed event. He will be dethroned and forced to share Mommy's and Daddy's time and attention. Since he's no longer the one and only object of your affection, he fears the total withdrawal of your love, and it likely will reflect in his behavior.

Put yourself in his shoes

Imagine that your spouse announces, "Darling, I love you more than you can imagine. Nevertheless, my high school girlfriend is moving in with us. I will be with you Monday, Wednesday, and Friday and with her Tuesday, Thursday, and Saturday. I'll rest on Sunday."

You'd be furious and outraged, jealousy spewing from your pores. You'd go from tears to tantrums; plotting ways of ejecting such a traitor from your household. Although siblings are generally accepted better than polygamy, the feelings associated with both sets of circumstances are similar. Be sensitive to the emotional roller coaster ride your firstborn will experience—love, protection, care, excitement, and curiosity one minute, and anger, jealousy, resentment, and fear of loss of love the next.

When a sibling comes along, the older child doesn't envision a potential playmate. He doesn't consider the possibility of a lifetime relationship with a person he may end up knowing longer and better than anyone else. Instead, he sees an intruder disrupting and interfering with his established life.

Softening the blow

Before your second child is born, include your firstborn as you prepare for the new baby. Let him help fold blankets, diapers, and pajamas. Include him as you set up the nursery. Explain what you are doing and why. By doing so, you communicate by your words and actions that he'll continue to belong in his family.

Although it's important to read stories about life with a new baby, there is simply no way to prepare the older child for the new set of emotions that will surface. Some children have an easier time than others when a new baby sister or brother is born, but it's important to be on guard.

But you're my mommy!

After the birth of their second child, a couple reported that when their 2½-year-old son saw his mother nurse his newborn sister for the first time, he asked, "Who's *her* mommy?"

This little boy's parents thought they had prepared the older child for the arrival of a sibling, but until he actually witnessed the baby in his mother's arms, it wasn't real. It was simply unfathomable to him that his mommy could be someone else's mommy, too.

Firstborn children expect one-to-one correspondence between themselves and their mother to be permanent. Children come up with unique solutions to solve the problem at hand. Because one child's Grandma and Grandpa obviously liked the new baby so much, he thought they should take her home. Many children suggest sending the infant back to the hospital. Parents need only respond:

"The baby lives here with us. She's a member of our family. We love you and we love your sister, too."

When it's apparent that your child is experiencing a new emotion, put words to it:

"I see you're interested in the baby. He's interested in you, too."

"It looks like you're feeling jealous. I'll put the baby down and hold you now."

"I can see that the baby's crying makes you worried. She's hungry; I'm going to feed her."

Accept the full range of your child's feelings, but if his behavior turns obnoxious or hurtful, stop it immediately. One child actually walked across the keyboard of the piano, another punched his mother in the arm. Some firstborn children attempt to poke, pinch, or punch their new brother or sister. They simply can't control their actions. The confusing mixture of emotions manifests itself in these aggressive attacks.

Define boundaries

You need to make it clear that aggression toward the new baby is not acceptable. More important, you must recognize that the responsibility for keeping the baby safe from her older sibling lies squarely with you. Be ready to separate your children, if necessary, and be right there to teach the older one to pat, never pound, the baby. As soon as parents demonstrate that they still have time for the older child, life gets easier. It can take three weeks to three months for the older child to fully accept the fact that he must now share his parents with a sibling. As parents, you must dig deep to create new attitudes and approaches to make sibling relationships work. The next stumbling block occurs when the baby starts to crawl. Now the interloper is not merely a source of emotional competition, but also a source of competition for toys. The crawler is a pesky irritant that knocks over block buildings and squeals with glee as she dismantles a train set. There *will* be screaming!

ReFeReEiNg
SiBlInG sQuAbBlEs

Who hit whom?
One mom describes the relationship between her daughters:
"My nine-year-old is very jealous and feels her six-year-old sister
gets all the attention. They argue a lot and have started hitting
each other. The older one claims the younger one starts it, but
I'm not always there to see what happens. My nine-year-old often
gets quite upset, cries, and throws things at her younger sister."

Parents with more than one child should tackle such sibling skirmishes
from three angles:
- First, create a strategy so you know what to do when children fight.
- Second, do everything possible to minimize the natural rivalry that
exists between siblings.
- Third, do what you can to provide opportunities for siblings to
build their relationship.

When siblings fight, the instigator is irrelevant. In fact, it was YOU who
really started the animosity when you gave birth to your second child!
One child may throw a dirty look, the other might clobber the one
who gave the dirty look. Although such aggressive behavior must be
stopped, blaming one child or the other usually makes sibling relations
worse. By the time a child is twelve months old, he knows what to do
to instigate an altercation with an older sibling. It's in your best interests
as a parent, therefore, and in the best interests of your children, to
reprimand equally when fighting erupts.

Tips for success

As fights break out—and they will—try not to respond the same way each time. You don't want to become the predictable third player in each fight. Depending on the situation, jump between these options:

1. Step in and stop the battle. Choose this tactic when one child is unmercifully bullying, teasing, or hurting the other, or when it's the fifth fight of the day and you've simply had enough.

Don't let this be your only tactic, or you'll rob your children of the opportunity to resolve their own differences.

2. Teach skills for managing conflict. Suggest strategies, such as trading, using timers, and taking turns. You're the arbitrator, helping your children peacefully resolve their own conflicts by compromising, negotiating, and working to solve the problem.

You can't always go this route because there are just too many disputes between siblings. You'll burn yourself out trying to resolve every one.

3. Allow children to manage the conflict themselves. Even if the older sibling is clearly taking advantage of (but not hurting) the younger, stay out of it. How else will the younger one learn to stand up for herself?

Don't ignore every battle, though. Sometimes your children need you to step in.

4. Use proximity control. Stand nearby and simply observe the verbal altercation. Your presence provides a calming influence and you're close enough to get involved if the battle comes to blows.

Sibling fights go from physical battles to screaming matches until that breakthrough moment when kids can discuss and resolve their differences peacefully. You must put a stop to physical aggression, but there's actually a positive side to the bickering: Verbal debates help siblings develop a sense of fairness. Those thousands of interactions that make you crazy give your children, right in their own home, an opportunity to learn social justice and to see things from someone else's perspective.

Same-sex siblings born close together exemplify the best and worst of sibling relations. They'll be buddies, best friends, and playmates, but also fierce competitors. Children of the opposite sex and those born three or more years apart also fight and can be rivals, but the tension is less pronounced.

A three-year-old has moved beyond the turbulent toddler period and is on the road to developing a life of his own. He goes to preschool and enjoys spending the afternoon with Grandma. Siblings of the opposite sex may enjoy some of the same activities, but they also involve themselves in activities that are of no interest to their brother or sister, thus reducing competition and making life a lot easier on the home front.

Minimizing Rivalry

Rivalry seems to be built into the sibling relationship. It's not enough that brothers and sisters fight with one another—they also compete for resources. Parents, and all that they provide—including food, objects, time, interest, and attention—are the resources. While children's fights evolve from physical battles to verbal arguments to learning how to negotiate and compromise their disagreements, rivalry may exist forever for some siblings. Knowing this, there's a lot that you can do to help minimize natural sibling rivalry.

Avoid the fairness trap

Every parent tries to be fair. If you're buying a new toy truck for your three-year-old, you naturally want to pick up a little something to appease your five-year-old. But if the older brother needs new soccer shoes, there's no need to buy little brother new shoes or anything else. If you do, you'll find yourself in the fairness trap. It's impossible to make everything equal for everybody all the time. If you try, the minute you slip up, your kids point it out, "You're not being fair. He got new shoes and I didn't. What do I get?" It's best to give possessions, time, and attention according to need and interest. On a daily basis things may not be fair between siblings, but if you are confident that in the long run you're being fair to your children, you'll prevent getting caught in the fairness trap.

Watch out for comparisons

There's no way to avoid comparing your children to each other, but voicing your comparisons will antagonize sibling relations. Siblings naturally compare themselves to each other—they don't need parents chiming in. Saying, "Why can't you be more like your brother? He got all As," doesn't motivate the less-academic one to study harder. It only helps to build resentment.

Each child seeks to carve out his unique spot in the family, so if one is academic, the other might relish being mediocre. You can talk about striving to reach a certain standard of achievement, but keep your comments about how each child is doing to private conversations.

Resist labels

In the same way, avoid labels. Saying, "She's my athlete" could hinder the other from being the athlete she's supposed to be. Such declarations might prompt your child to think: "Why try when my sister is the athletic one?" Saying, "He's the family troublemaker" only places that child in a role that's difficult to escape. Each child behaves well some of the time and acts up at other times.

Accept negative feelings

When a child says, "I hate my brother," your natural reaction is, "You don't hate your brother; he's your best friend for life." Although it's important to put a stop to using the "hate" word, a better response is, "I know you're angry at your brother because he interferes when you're playing with your buddies, but it's not OK to hate him."

Siblings feel love and loyalty toward each other, mixed with irritation, resentment, and jealousy. You can't squelch those feelings, so validate them and they'll dissolve. Just don't allow any accompanying negative behavior: "You can be jealous of your sister, but it's not OK to hit her."

Offer your time to each child

One of the best buffers against sibling rivalry is spending time with each child every day. This doesn't require a lot of time, but it needs to be positive and focused on the uniqueness and strengths of each child.

Develop a "tucking in bed" ritual: "I'm so glad you're my child. Today you were so helpful getting a diaper for baby Sam. Also, thanks for drawing that picture while I talked on the phone to Grandma. I love your eyes. I'm so happy you're learning to ride a bicycle."

Forget favoritism

Your favoritism of one child over another does not serve siblings well. In some homes there's a designated favorite child. In other homes children compete daily for that position. If you find yourself favoring one child over another, keep those feelings to yourself and do not let your children know. No child would thrive knowing he's less favored. Each child has unique attributes, so cherish those qualities and let that child—and that child alone—know of them.

real life parenting

A mom's dilemma

One mom described this rare sibling interaction:

"My boys, ages six and eight, sat on the floor side-by-side, building cars peacefully with Legos. The older one actually dug through the Lego box for the exact piece his younger brother needed. The younger spontaneously commented that he thought his brother's car was 'way cool.' They showed interest in what the other was building, and exchanged ideas and construction strategies. Then, even more amazing, they decided to combine their efforts by constructing a garage to house their automobiles.

"I wanted to step in with a reinforcing compliment, saying something like, 'It's so nice to see you two playing without fighting.' I hesitated, and decided that doing so might alert them to the positive nature of their interaction, and a physical or verbal fight might quickly erupt."

The mom's question: "Should I have complimented them? What can I do to support the relationship between my boys? Most of the time I'm refereeing everything from wrestling matches to disputes over possessions, violations of property infringement, and various forms of unfairness. I'd much rather be doing something proactive so in the long run they'll end up being friends for life."

Answer: While there are no magic tricks for creating instant sibling harmony, parents aren't powerless. You can promote positive relationships that will result in fond memories of growing up together and increase the chance for life-long sibling closeness.

Nurturing the sibling Relationship

When harmony hits, hold your parent tongue

As this mom so wisely realized, when a sibling pair is playing or interacting positively, it's not the time to blurt out, "Boy, I really like seeing the two of you getting along so well!" Doing so might destroy the moment and disrupt the positive nature of the interaction. Instead, when tucking each in bed that night, offer a compliment.

Offer a prop

Another approach is to extend play by offering a prop appropriate to the children's activity. If your children are engaged in a pretend tea party, fill the tea pot with real milk and give them some real cookies, thereby extending the play and the relationship between sister and brother.

Underline positive qualities

When siblings exhibit desirable qualities toward each other, such as cooperation, generosity, compassion, or honesty, reinforce the behavior by saying, "I notice you're putting a Band-Aid on your brother's knee (for now, leave out the part about pushing him down on the sidewalk). That's showing compassion." Or, "I saw you give your little sister half your cookie (never mind that older sister gave herself the bigger half). That was very kind."

Step near and play, too

Sometimes when your children are playing a game or building with Legos, you might sense tension brewing between them. Without a reprimand, simply step in and play the game or build a Lego house, too, moving the sibling interaction in a positive direction and sidestepping an explosion of emotions between the two.

Enhance playtimes

Notice when your children are getting along. Is it when they're playing computer games, baking cookies, or playing imaginatively? Is it when they're romping around outside or building a fort under a tree or the dining room table? When you identify what your children enjoy doing together, make every effort to provide more of these opportunities. When they're involved in a positive activity, they're building their relationship separately from you. Isn't that what you want?

The sibling relationship lasts for life. Parents can do a lot to maximize the positive aspects of this relationship despite the rivalry that occurs along the way.

ONE CAN BE WONDERFUL

When you think of an only child, do you see a lonely, selfish outsider who is spoiled, demanding, acts too much like an adult and, therefore, is socially handicapped among his peers?

These notions are passé. Statistics show that only children are often leaders who are intelligent high achievers. They typically enjoy their own company, as they've learned to entertain themselves.

Many parents today choose to have just one child. Why? Many career women wait longer to get married, and after the birth of a child continue to work outside the home. Reliable birth control methods prevent unplanned births. Economic realities—the high cost of child care and child rearing—deter some parents from having more than one child. Of course, some women have physical problems conceiving and carrying a child to term, so these moms feel blessed with their only child.

A parent with more than one child may look with envy at parents who chose to have only one child, thinking that they're infinitely smarter than those with two, three, and four children. When your kids are bickering and fighting, when you're feeling tired and torn between the needs of one child over another, your thoughts might wistfully drift to only one pair of shoes to tie, one child to drive to baseball practice, one child to tutor the multiplication tables and one set of teen driving lessons.

Blow the old wives' tales out of the water

Regardless of your reasons for having an only child, there is lots of positive evidence supporting your choice.

Forget the old wives' tales!
- Only children do not necessarily show signs of being unstable.
- Studies show that adult-aged only children are happy in their career choices, lifestyles, health, and hobbies.
- Only children aren't significantly lonelier than others.
- Only children perform well on intelligence and achievement tests.
- The self-esteem and mental health of only children do not differ consistently from children with siblings.
- Only children tend to express a high degree of maturity and social sensitivity at an early age.
- The only child is never dethroned by the not so blessed birth of the second child.

That being said, watch out for the disadvantages:

1. You might expect this child to be everything to you. With three children, one might be the good student, another the athlete, another the social butterfly. Parents of an only child might unrealistically and unfairly expect her to be all of these.

2. Your child does not have siblings around to learn to share, trade, and negotiate. It's up to you to create opportunities for your child to regularly play and socialize with neighborhood or school friends.

3. You might be tempted to think of your child as a miniature adult. Many parents of only children expect their child to behave more maturely than is realistic for children. Your child will receive the full extent of your attention and care, but also the full force of your discipline. Be careful to avoid being overly demanding and critical.

4. You might tend to be overprotective. It's difficult for any parent to allow a child to manage certain situations and it's even more difficult for parents of only children. They tend to go overboard shielding their child from the school of bumps and bruises.

Along with overprotecting comes the inclination to over-parent. One adult remembered the time his teacher assigned a train report in school. Because they wanted to help him Mom and Dad took over. They went to the library, wrote off for brochures and pamphlets to several railroad companies, made a miniature train layout, and organized a ride on Amtrak. They even wrote most of the report. This child was overwhelmed and over-parented. He knew better than his parents that it was supposed to be his report, not theirs. Be alert to when you might be interfering in your child's life and know when it's beneficial to back off.

Chapter 3
Watch 'em Grow

THE SIX STAGES OF BAKING COOKIES

When you're a new parent, you're so busy changing diapers, nursing, rocking, singing, and cooing that it's nearly impossible to think ahead to the time when your helpless baby will be a toddler throwing a tantrum, much less a teenager negotiating a curfew. And it's even harder to imagine your future role in those situations. With every stage of your child's development, your parenting approach should change to accommodate new responsibilities and challenges.

Take baking cookies: it's a completely different experience with your infant than it is with your teenager. And whatever your child's stage of development, it's impossible to know how the cookies will turn out. If you mix the following advice into your parenting recipe, however, the process will be more palatable.

Infancy: Parent on call

When your child is an infant, she demands and deserves instant gratification. She's helpless. If you try to put her off, she has no internal resources to call on to manage herself. Your role is that of loving slave. Cookie baking, or anything else for that matter, must wait until your baby is asleep or, at least, content.

When she's hungry, you nurse her *immediately*; if she needs to cling, you carry her until her need for physical contact is satisfied; if she's too warm or cold, you busy yourself adjusting her clothing and the room temperature until she's comfy. By attending to her needs, you build trust, helping her understand that whenever she's needy, you'll be there. Your baby thrives under such responsive care.

It's also up to you to engage your infant in social interaction, baby style. This includes smiling and cooing, babbling and singing. You may try to pass baby off to Grandma but often it's you, and you alone, who baby demands. She likes mommy's and daddy's voices and smiling faces best.

Toddler years: Parent as bodyguard

As your toddler's bodyguard, you're responsible not only for her safety but also for planning recreational activities and nurturing her. Your job now is to provide the opportunity for your child to explore and experiment, while making sure she remains safe. So cookie baking is great fun for both of you, as long as you don't care how the cookies turn out—or even whether they get made at all.

She learns and is happiest when copying you and will likely want to be right by your side, tasting, stirring, and insisting, "Me do it." Set your toddler on a stool, and give her a bowl with a few ingredients of her own to mix. Expect a mess, and for safety's sake, keep an eye on her to avoid danger.

You can almost hear your toddler's internal developmental clock dinging for independence. This independent streak may tell her to dump liquid soap into the cookie batter. When you say "no", don't expect her to comply. It's your job to provide the control she lacks by taking the soap away. Then prepare yourself for her emotional meltdown.

Your frustration level may rise, too, but it's up to you to remain calm and not lose patience. Once her temper tantrum subsides, continue making those cookies. You may wish you had spent the afternoon playing on your toddler's terms and buying cookies from the bakery, but take heart: Life smoothes out as your child approaches her third year.

Preschool years: Parent as teacher

Preschool age is the time when your child learns quickly and eagerly by emulating you. Preschoolers relish completing a task just as you request. When you say, "Pour this cup of flour in that bowl," she will do so happily. Whether it's putting toys away, getting dressed, or learning to use scissors, glue, and magic markers, she will learn best when you teach in small steps, recognizing degrees of progress along the way: "Good for you. You put your shirt on all by yourself. Now put on your pants. I'll watch." Language and the acquisition of self-control enable the teaching process.

As you and your preschooler frost your heart-shaped cookies, yours may be perfect, hers less so; but she doesn't notice. She simply benefits from the process. But if you leave the room, she might take the initiative to add green food coloring to the pink frosting. With the frosting now gray, what do you do?

Your natural reaction may be irritation, and you might be tempted to reprimand her for proceeding without permission. But there's no need to pour on guilt—you'll take away her initiative. With a measure of calm, talk about what she did, discussing what happens when green mixes with pink.

You'll often see your preschooler reenacting her experiences through imaginative play. Your job is to provide the tools and a playmate for such dramatic play to unfold. By doing so, she resists the activity through her mental processes. If you give her some empty food color bottles and a bowl, you might see her pretend to reexperience what happens when she mixes pink and green.

School-age years: Parent as mentor

During the early school years, ages six to eleven, your child takes charge of her projects, but she still needs you by her side, coaching her. When baking cookies, you become her mentor. Children of this age may not know that "T" means tablespoon and "t" means teaspoon. So go ahead, and gently engage her intellect: "Before you get started, let's talk about the abbreviations used in baking."

If your child goofs up as the project gets underway, you need only say, "That's too bad. Would you like me to help you fix it?" You walk a fine line here. It's important to offer information and assistance, but do so without taking over or making your child feel inadequate.

School-aged kids need to take charge of much more than cookie baking: bedrooms, allowances, homework, computer work, and hobbies all become part of the school-age domain. This switch from parent-in-charge to child-in-charge is a tough one for many parents. Don't give up parenting; instead, move from your former role of teacher to mentor with grace. Your child needs you in the kitchen, but you don't need to direct every teaspoon and tablespoon she adds to the batter.

Tweens: Parents as secret police

During the years between twelve and fourteen your child's body goes through puberty. She'll be self-absorbed, introspective, and most likely won't be interested in making cookies at all. But because she's growing so rapidly, she may sit and eat your entire batch without any consideration for anyone else.

The youngster is caught in the middle between childhood and the teen years. The strong pull of the pop culture will pressure her to emulate teen-oriented media stars in her behavior, clothes, hair, and possibly piercings and tattoos. Allow some of it within reason, but stress the importance of modesty (yes, even with boys) and disallow permanent body disfiguring that she may regret in the future.

Expect to be outraged one day, perplexed the next, and frequently worried if you can safely monitor your child through this difficult and somewhat bizarre stage of development.

You'll weather the emotional storm of the tween years more easily if you keep track of your child. Know where she is and whom she's with at all times. Chauffeur kids around, invite their friends into your home, and provide your tempting homemade cookies. Zip your lip in their presence, but listen closely to their conversations. If you sense danger, step up to the parenting plate and address the issue in private with your child.

Develop your sense of humor and don't show cowardice. Know when to muster the courage to prevent your tween from doing something you both will regret.

Teenage years: Parents as spectator

When your teenager bakes cookies, she doesn't even want you in the kitchen. On her final push for independence, the teen's internal timer is ticking down, alerting her that in a few years she'll be on her own. She begins practicing for adulthood now.

It's your job to hold back and let your teen decide things for herself: Will she take French or Spanish, or join the debate club or baseball team? And when she's baking cookies, even if she substitutes baking powder for baking soda, she needs to complete this task and many similar ones independently of your well-intentioned advice.

You'll garner the most success when you offer objective, succinct pieces of information: "I smell cookies burning." "If you get a ticket, your insurance rate will go up."

Support your teen's push for independence as long as it's safe. If you say no to a weekend at the ocean with friends without parental supervision, tell your teen, "It's only because I love you so much. As a responsible parent, I can't allow it."

Also learn what you can and can't control. You control the TV, the telephone, the keys to the car, and the stereo volume. You can't control your teen's thinking, attitude, emotions, or eating and sleeping habits, so don't waste your energy trying.

Teens will argue every point from curfews to political philosophy. When negotiating curfews, if you or your teen reaches the boiling point, end the conversation. When it comes to political philosophy, sexuality, and values, go ahead and have your say, but understand that even the most well-meaning parent is considered to be an adversary to a teenager.

Although there are no cookie-cutter kids and no guaranteed recipe for success, this method will allow you to build the parent-child relationship while nurturing your child's development.

If your child could sit right down and write you a letter explaining his behavior, here's what she'd likely want you to know about nurturing her through each stage of development.

A letter from your infant
(0 to 18 months)

Dear Mommy and Daddy,

More than anything, I need your responsive care. I need you to cuddle me and to let me cling. When you caress me for as long as I want, I feel secure. I won't be dependent and clingy forever, and don't worry, I'm too tiny to spoil.

I know I'm demanding, but realize that before I was born I was in the perfect environment of the womb. Now I've been thrust into the world, so for a while, since I'm a baby, you need to do all you can to recreate that environment by satisfying my every need.

Once I'm fed and changed and cuddled and rocked, then you can put me down and I'll sleep so you can rest or get some of your work done. When I'm distressed I need you to pick me up ASAP and comfort me because I can't comfort myself.

By offering me attentive care, I grow to trust that you'll be there to care for me. I won't worry about who will feed, hold, and keep me warm; I'll relax knowing you're nearby.

From the day I'm born, please talk to me. It might seem silly at first but go ahead and talk. No one needs to teach you how; you'll just know to speak using a high-pitched voice. In only a few months I'll respond by smiling, cooing, and babbling back.

But also notice when I've had enough. Sometimes people bombard me with stimulating talk and toys. I like it sometimes, but when you get the idea that I've had enough, please stop. Since I can't talk, you need to watch me. I'll let you know what I need!

Also realize that from birth I can see, smell, hear, feel, and taste. The most important sensory connections I make are with you. It's your face, scent, and voice I like best. At just one week old, I know your face from a stranger's. Pretty amazing, aren't I?

I can also copy movements you make with your mouth. So even though you and I may look ridiculous, stick your tongue out at me, and then I'll mimic you.

Not too long after I'm born, I'll start to use combinations of my senses. I'll see your face and at the same time smell your skin. This combination feels right. I'll feel the rhythm of you rocking me and hear your voice singing to that rhythm.

When the dog barks, the phone rings, the TV blares, and people talk and move around, it's easy for me to feel overwhelmed. That's when I need you to take me away from it all for quiet rocking and singing to bring my senses back in sync.

Mommy, since you're usually the one who cares for me, it seems I like you more. It's only because you read my cues for care quickly. Daddy, I like you too, you're just different. You smell, feel, look, sound, and even taste different than Mommy does. You're more playful. I like you to bounce me around, but don't toss me in the air. My brain is fragile. Daddy, know that you can comfort me when I'm upset. Mommy seems to do it easily, but I know that you can do it, too.

Your face and all it can do—move and make noises—hold my interest, but you might decide to buy a few toys. A baby-safe ball that rolls and bounces will fascinate me while supporting my fierce curiosity about how objects move.

Whatever toys you provide—a mobile, a jack-in-the-box, or a touchy-feely turtle—pick out ones that you can safely alter from time to time or ones that have a variety of textures, sights and movements. I like familiar objects that change slightly. That way I won't be bored or over-stimulated.

When you put me on the floor to stretch and wiggle on my tummy, please gently touch my face, toes, and hands, and talk to me. Your gentle touch and interest let me know you love me.

Feeling unconditional love from the beginning, I'll learn to love others. I need both my mommy and daddy to be the best parents they can be. I deserve this. You are the most important people in my life. With your love and caring attention, I'm off to a good start reaching my potential.

Your Baby

A letter from your toddler
(18 months to 3 years)

Dear Mommy and Daddy,

I'm on the go with no inner controls and I like to make things happen—turn on lights, push TV buttons, and flush toilets. My curiosity drives me and I put myself in harm's way much of the time. You may think you've perfectly child-proofed our house, but I'll discover places and things you never thought I could reach or would be interested in. I need your protection from these dangers.

Now that I'm a good walker, I want to master climbing and jumping. Please provide me with a safe place to do this, and be sure to keep your eyes on me at all times.

When you're fixing dinner, I like to hang on your leg to see what you're doing. I know it's annoying but I can't help myself. I want to be right by your side.

I know you wish I'd go off to play by myself, but I'm persistent. Why not get me a sturdy stool? I'll be happy if I can climb up on it all by myself, tear apart a little lettuce, look out the window, and play with water at the sink.

My mission is to satisfy my curiosity and become competent in and around my home. You can help by putting out on floors, tables, or in special cupboards some objects for me to see and then touch, taste, listen to, and smell. I learn by using all of my senses. I'd also like a vehicle to ride and a cart to push. Demanding, aren't I?

I'm trying to understand that things and people still exist even when I can't see them. That's why I love to play peek-a-boo, hide-and-seek, and chase.

When you come back from shopping, why don't you take the paper bags and load them up with safe household items, and I'll carry them around and dump them out. This may look unproductive to you, but I'll do it again and again and stay happy and engaged.

I'm a copycat so give me a toothbrush, comb, and washcloth. I'll begin to learn good habits while imitating you. I'd also like the same everyday items that you use, such as a key chain loaded with keys, an old telephone, or a computer keyboard.

Prepare yourself: you'll sometimes hear me say, "No, no, no," "Go away," or "Leave me alone." Don't panic, Mommy. I've just discovered that I have a mind of my own and I'm going overboard to prove it. When you can, go along with my demands. If I don't want to wear my coat and it's not freezing, let me get in the car without it.

There will come a day when I move toward a forbidden object. I'll look you straight in the eye as if to say, "I am interested in the lamp cord. How do you feel about me touching it?" You'll be thinking, "He's done this before with the very same cord. He must know he's not supposed to touch it, so why in the world is he testing me again?"

I'm not only interested in the forbidden cord, but also fascinated with the fact that we have conflicting interests. Hey, don't take it personally! I'm not being defiant on purpose. I just need to know consistently that we have a conflict of interest about the lamp cord and that you'll protect me from its dangers.

Watch out for my temper. You're really going to see it now that I'm a toddler. When you stop me from doing what I want to do, my temper will flare. Don't pay too much attention to me, but don't desert me either. Just say something like, "Boy, you're really angry," and not much more. Please don't get mad yourself. When I'm out of control, I need you to stay calm.

Don't let this independent side of me fool you; I'm really just one step away from being a baby. When you're frustrated and don't know what to do with me, get my blanket and read me my favorite book or sit down on the floor and watch me play, give a play-by-play description of what I'm doing. You can play, too, but remember, I'm in charge.

Please help me move gracefully through this taxing period of my life. Once I'm preschool-aged, if you've done your job, I'll leave the challenges of toddlerhood behind. I promise!

Your Toddler

A letter from your preschool-aged child
(3 to 5 years)

Dear Mommy and Daddy,

My imagination is vivid, so when it comes to play and learning, fewer toys mean more to me. I don't need toys that replicate a house, airport, or grocery store, I can create my own spaces with tape, boxes, paper, and marking pens. Watch me play and you'll realize that my imagination—not the toy I'm holding—dictates what I do.

Blocks, dress-up clothes, a doctor kit, bandages, pencils, paper, chalkboard, calculator, play computer, and clipboard help bring my ideas to life. I enjoy toy cars and trucks, but then I'll use blocks to build roads, garages, and towns. With a doll I have a patient, a student, and a secretary for when I play doctor, school, and office.

Here's what works best for me. Suppose after a trip to the market I say, "Dad, I want to make a grocery store." That's your signal to step in and help out. Save some used food cartons and cans, get out some grocery bags. I'll use a box for the cash register and make my own play money and credit and debit cards.

Once the grocery store is set up, let me keep it up for a few days. As the play goes on day by day, add items to the store to enhance my playtime.

As I play, I'm putting together mental pictures of everything I've observed when we go shopping: commerce, nutrition, food supply, and more. I'm interested in becoming competent as I come and go into various environments. When I'm playing, I'm learning, and it's not a frivolous pastime—it's what we preschool-aged children are programmed to do.

I also need a playmate my own age. With a friend, I can practice sharing, trading, and taking turns. We may fight and bicker, and when we do, just step in and help us solve the problem. My friend and I build on one another's ideas as we negotiate, problem solve, and play through various imaginative situations.

I really like to help with tasks around the house. Even though you can do any job faster and better, I feel important when I can feed the cat, set the table, and put my dirty clothes in the hamper. But I need you to oversee, prompt, and remind me what to do.

When I build a fort, complete a puzzle, or draw a picture, let me know that you're proud of me. When I share toys and then put them away, let me know you're pleased.

I'm eager and ready to learn to dress myself, brush my teeth, put items where they belong, and prepare to leave the house with my coat and shoes on. My mind and body are ready to master these daily tasks, so expect me to complete them and do so consistently until they become positive habits that I will have learnt to do automatically.

Sure, I may test your rules, but family rules are still important to me. If you really want me to take my shoes off when I come in the house, enforce this rule consistently. Don't be wishy-washy and change your mind when I complain, whine, or pout.

Just don't make too many rules all at once. Gradually teach me more and more rules that are important to the family. You can even say, "In our family we sit at the table for 15 minutes to eat our dinner." I enjoy belonging to the family, so I'll usually go along with what we all do together.

Turn the TV off even though I may gripe. Deep inside I know I'm better off with less screen time as there are so many other fun things to do.

Please take my ideas seriously and don't laugh at me. I have lots of initiative. If I can't use my ideas or if you put them down, I'll feel unimportant and discouraged, and my ideas may stop coming. You don't want this to happen, do you?

I need you to stop me when I get out of control. Don't let me hit others or damage anything, but do give me words to express my frustration.

Even though I'm growing bigger, I still like to sit on your lap every day while you read to me. There's no need to take away my beloved blanket or teddy bear. I won't take them to college, but for now I still need their comfort.

Your Preschooler

A letter from your school-aged child
(6 to 11 years)

Dear Mommy and Daddy,

Even though I'm involved with a new life just beyond the confines of home—school, activities, and friends—my family is still important. In a few years, once puberty hits, I'll question everything you do and you'll easily embarrass me by how you dress and what you say. But for now, take advantage of the fact that I'm eager to hear your opinion and learn from your point of view.

If you don't let me know your values, ideas, and perspectives, I'll search for understanding from peers, the media and, of course, my teachers. These influences can lead me positively and appropriately, or negatively and inappropriately. Mom and Dad, it's so easy for you to exert your influence, and it's important and necessary that you do.

If my friends seem obnoxious, help me find a peer group—through music, dance, religion, scouting, and sports—that fits with the kind of friends and interests that you'd like me to have. If TV, the Internet, movies, video games, and DVDs portray characters with values that don't sit well with you, limit my screen time. But also provide books and movies that do fit with the values you hold dear.

I prefer activities that feed into my need to be industrious. School provides one avenue but I need more after school, too. I yearn for projects such as cooking, gardening, and using the computer to help me become competent in the world in which I live.

When I'm assigned a project for the upcoming science fair at school, I'll be determined to complete it independently using my own ideas. But realistically, I need your help to succeed, because what I visualize will be hard for me to translate into a product that works the way I'd like.

I need you to show you're interested, while coaching me to get the job done.

I love making hideouts where my friends and I can meet to form secret clubs. Don't feel threatened when a sign reads, "Private. Keep out!" I'm only letting you know that I'm in this wonderful period where I thrive when playing with friends, yet my family and parents are still important.

I'd like to throw my own birthday party. I'll plan all the games and activities myself. Keep an eye out—I may need your help—but don't take over and dominate. It's my party, not yours.

I want to arrange and decorate my own bedroom. It may be difficult for you to accept this, but I don't like ballerina wallpaper. Hey, I'm a soccer player, remember?

I love being involved in establishing and observing family rituals. If there's a holiday tradition you'd like our family to take on, now is the time to try it. If you wait until I'm a teenager, I'll probably resist.

I thrive on competition with friends, whether on the playfield or when playing video games.

I'm interested in the community beyond our neighborhood, and I'm eager for safe adventures away from home. That could mean a bike ride around the neighborhood, going to a convenience store for candy, or traveling on a plane to visit cousins. I hope you will allow a few such adventures, and I understand how hard it is in a society that you fear is dangerous.

Once I'm ten years old, I'll want to learn skills for taking care of myself in the real world. Your job is to lay a net for safety while allowing me to strike out in the broader environment beyond home.

While I'm grounded in reality, I still keep one foot in fantasy. Wizardry, magic, and the supernatural fit nicely into my imaginative life. Books and games that involve science fiction and fantasy themes hold much fascination and intrigue.

I still like and need your time and attention. Don't let this age slip by without taking advantage of the fact that I still like you and am open to your influence. Before you know it, I'll be tweenager, trying to grow up before I'm ready.

Your School-aged Kid

A letter from your tween
(12 to 14 years)

Dear Mom and Dad,

Brace yourself. Now that I'm between eleven and
fourteen, you're about to witness one of the most
drastic metamorphoses since I sprouted from infant to
toddler. And the similarities don't stop there.

Remember my temper tantrums? You'll see similar
eruptions of anger again. Remember lines like, "Leave
me alone, I do it my way!"? Well, they're back, only
now I'll be saying, "Get out of my face!"

Some days you'll feel like denouncing parenthood
altogether! Please don't, I need you. I just can't let
you know it.

This transition between childhood and full-grown
adolescence will hit our relationship hard. Try to
understand the changes I'm facing. My raging
hormones and fast-growing body are shocking
adjustments for me to make.

And then there's my expanding school load with more
academic responsibility. Recess is over permanently.
But don't barge in the front door demanding
compliance and a sweet cooperative attitude. You'll only

alienate me. Instead, come in the back door with a low-key yet clear approach.

You'll be tempted to listen in on my phone calls and read notes and e-mails between my friends and me. You may even want to rifle through my backpack. Don't do it! You'll only make our relationship worse. If I'm in trouble at school, with friends, or with the law, and snooping is needed for my safety, put me on notice.

For now, my friends seem more important than you. To become an adult, I must push away from you. My friends help me bridge the gap between dependence on you, and independence as a grown-up.

I won't come home from school with details about my day. Instead, I'll be on my cell phone or instant messaging.

The social scene changes daily at school. One day I'll be popular and the next I may feel disliked and rejected. Please make home a safe retreat for me. Rejection from both friends and parents is too much for me to bear.

I'm riding an emotional roller coaster. One minute I'll be overly controlled as I put together a class project, the next I'll be screaming because someone drank one of my favorite sodas.

My growth spurts will be dramatic—hands and feet first, then legs and arms, with the torso eventually catching up. Of course, I'll be developing sexually as well. Provide me with information about my changing body even if it's embarrassing for us both.

With all the other changes taking place, it might seem that my mind has stopped working. My schoolwork might suffer. Don't panic. Once I settle into my new body, friends, and school, my mind will catch up.

I'm getting acquainted with my new body and emotions and sometimes, I simply can't manage the changes gracefully. I need nurturing but it will take an approach far different from when I was little.

Here are some ways:
• Provide me with lots of nutritious food and don't bug me about how much or when I eat. If I'm obese or severely underweight, seek help from a professional.

• When I sit down to eat, sit down too. Gossip a little about the office or family, or talk about an outrageous news story. Open yourself up to me, and I may do the same for you.

• Develop and use your sense of humor. If you don't have a knack for injecting humor into tense situations, give it a try anyway; it often saves the day.

• Compliment or notice something about my appearance each day. Don't ignore my purple fingernail polish, call attention to it. "Look at your fingernails. I'm amazed at that color." If you fail to notice the purple nails today, you might see purple hair tomorrow.

• Let me keep my bedroom as I choose. Don't allow black paint, risqué posters, or dirty dishes, but otherwise back off when it comes to bedroom controls. Try to remember it's my space.

• Keep track of me. I'm going to push my boundaries, so do extend them, but make it clear that family members keep track of one another. Tell me it's not because you want to control my life, just reassure me it's because you love me so much.

• Show up at my school or sport events. I want you there—just don't call any attention to yourself or me—no high fives or hugs. Wear beige and keep your mouth shut.

I realize that you walk a fine parenting line while I'm a tweenager and that you won't always get it right.

Your Tween

A letter from your teen
(15 to 18 years)

Dear Mom and Dad,

What I really need from you is to understand what it's like to be a teenager. Just because I'm breaking away right now doesn't mean it will be forever. All the values you instilled during my growing-up years are still with me; they just lie sleeping right now while I do some questioning and rebelling.

One of the safest places for me to rebel is in the sanctity of my own room, which will most likely be a mess. Unless it's particularly unsanitary (sour milk in a cereal bowl or mildewing damp towels), allow it. When I move out after high school, I'll probably be reasonably neat. Right now my room is a better place to rebel than at school or in the community. I'll spend a lot of time in my room just thinking about life, so it'd be nice if you would provide some comfy pillows and a comforter to snuggle up in.

So much is going on with me right now. As a teenager my mind is expanding. At school I'm learning the advanced concepts of algebra and the metaphors and similes of poetry. My thinking is more sophisticated and flexible. I see the world from a broader perspective and have my own ideas about what I see and hear.

These mental attributes assist me at school but my thinking doesn't stop once I reach our front door. It's important that you listen to my opinions. Don't put me down and don't tune me out. But don't be afraid to engage in heated discussions either. Ask me questions and show interest in my interests. Let's have a spirited discussion about war and peace, taxes, and global warming—even if we differ.

If a battle gets too hot, end it. Just remember, disagreements and thought-provoking discussions actually keep us attached during these turbulent teen years.

Also understand my emotions are on a seesaw. Sometimes I'm up and sometimes I'm down. I pout and sulk, then it's over and I'm happy again. If I start yelling uncontrollably, stay near me or walk away, but don't throw me out of the house. I need to release my emotional energy. Be steady when I'm out of control. I've got to keep my emotions together at school and with my friends so sometimes I'll just explode at home. I won't always act like this; just remember I'm a teenager. My emotional outbursts or moodiness will pass.

I'll be argumentative and surly sometimes. It's only because I'm getting acquainted with my new body and set of emotions, and my new mind. I simply can't manage the changes gracefully.

Now let's talk about food. I'm hungry most of the time. Keep the refrigerator full, or better yet, let me go to the store and pick out the food I like. You might consider buying me a latte machine, yogurt maker, or a blender for smoothies.

Just because I'm as big as an adult doesn't mean that I have adult experience and judgment, so don't expect it. I still need information and advice delivered in sound bites. "Remember the speed limit is 60 miles an hour on the freeway; if you get a ticket you lose the privilege of driving the car." Once you've said it, realize that I heard it, and drop it. Don't expect me to say, "Thanks for the reminder, Dad, I really appreciate your concern." More likely, I'll scoff at you, roll my eyes, show my defiance, and then huff away.

Just because I'm obnoxious sometimes, don't push me away. I still need you. I still love you. I just can't come right out and say it.

If you're truly interested in my independence you'll provide me with a car. OK, so that's unlikely. How about a cell phone, my own computer programs, or an electronic keyboard?

Because it's really important for me to be accepted by my friends I need trendy clothing, jewelry, or a backpack that signals belonging to a peer group. Please allow me one set of concert tickets so a friend and I can prove that we can manage ourselves at the concert, unchaperoned.

Nurturing me requires supporting my need to be independent while keeping me safe and maintaining our relationship. I realize it's a tricky business being my parent and I do still love you.

Your Teen

CHAPTER 4

HEALTHY HABITS

LeArNiNg GoOd HaBiTs

Before giving birth you probably never realized just how much it takes to teach children good habits. Most likely you didn't even think of the fact that children best learn such habits during the preschool years. But that's the truth of the matter. Your job is to devote time when your kids are preschoolers, then those habits —washing hands after going to the potty, taking the plate from the table to the counter after eating, reading before falling asleep —will be in place. However, never get your hopes too high. Even if you've done your part, your children will most likely need reminders and prompting until they graduate from high school.

Bear in mind that children like instant gratification. They would prefer running outside to play rather than scraping their plate first; and they're impulsive so they want what they want when they want it. When they see a cookie they want to eat it immediately without saying "please" and then "thank you." These characteristics can work against your child's careful upbringing.

Yes, it takes time. Yes, you must again and again stop them from grabbing and gobbling a cookie while insisting they say "please" and "thank you" first. Yes, you must leave an NBA playoff game to oversee teeth brushing and then read a story or two. But by doing so, by the time they're in early elementary school, they'll be fairly independent when it comes to taking care of their personal daily habits.

Many hassles between parents and their elementary school-aged children center around kids who haven't learned to put toys away, to sleep through the night in their own room, and who don't come to the table when dinner's called. By guiding your children to come to the table when young, you avoid yelling at them to do so when older. They'll arrive automatically out of habit. Once a healthy habit is in place the bonus is that you'll have more energy to enjoy your children and your role as a nurturing parent.

You'll never call a routine "Boring" Again

Children rely even more so than adults on consistency and routine. In most homes at about 8p.m. the bedtime routine begins. Moms and dads conduct their own version of it by locating their child's beloved blanket, having him brush his teeth, go to the bathroom, and put on pajamas, reading a story, having him say a prayer, offering a kiss and a hug, turning on the night light, saying "good night," and closing the child's bedroom door. Parents conduct the routine with the hope that then the child will drift off to sleep.

When Mom or Dad seeks out the beloved blanket it triggers in the child's mind the rest of the steps in the bedtime routine. If parents attempt to change the routine or leave out one step, most children notice by offering a reminder or by boldly protesting.

Children rely on such routines because they make their life predictable. Think about what a child's day would be like if there were no routines in place—if mealtime, bedtime, and playtime didn't follow any schedule, and if people appeared and disappeared unpredictably. If this were the case, children would sit vigilantly waiting and wondering what's going to happen next and who's coming or going.

But don't worry and don't be too rigid either. Most homes run on reasonable schedules, and because most parents behave in a predictable fashion, children feel emotionally safe, which allows them to focus on learning, playing, and satisfying their curiosity.

Amazing as it may seem, children as young as five months can determine a sequence of events.

Morning mania

It's not only the bedtime routine that's important to young children, but also the "getting up in the morning routine" which includes dressing, eating breakfast, grooming, and positive interactions including cuddles and conversation with Mom or Dad. Then there's the "getting out the door to school or child-care routine" which includes one more trip to the bathroom, putting on shoes and coat, grabbing lunch and backpack, and climbing in the car seat.

Be on the lookout for negative elements that might seep into your daily routines. Let's say you're in the habit of calling your child three times to come to the dinner table and then the fourth time yelling at him. The yelling becomes part of the "coming to the dinner table routine" and the child grows to expect it. If Dad screams at a child each morning to put on his shoes, that scream becomes part of the "getting out the door routine."

When working to establish positive routines, your child needs you right there assisting and then guiding him through each step of getting dressed. Later he needs you to watch him and describe his positive action: "I saw you put on your shirt, now I'll watch you put on your pants." Because children are easily distracted, most need friendly one-word reminders until late adolescence when the child moves out of the family home.

After-dinner routine

The Blankeys established this after-dinner routine. Once everyone had helped with the dishes, the TV, computer, music players, Internet, and telephone remained off. Then the family gathered around the table for quiet reading and work time. When the children were toddlers and preschoolers, Mom and Dad read to the children or the children drew with pencils and paper, or they counted and sorted buttons, pennies, or small toys or objects.

Once the children started school and homework assignments began, the time and routine for them were already in place. There were no tears or tantrums because of a change of routine: The TV was already off and the time was set aside for homework with Mom and Dad available to help, monitor, or guide the children from one assignment to the next. Mom and Dad read their books or worked on their paper and pencil projects, writing notes or paying bills. As the children moved ahead in the school years, computer work was allowed and children could go off to their own bedrooms to work alone. If there were no homework assignments, the children were required to read.

This routine carried on through all the years until the kids one-by-one went off to college. The Blankeys had established a consistent routine of academic discipline. Music or sports practice occurred before, not after, dinner to avoid interfering with study time. It was high priority to the family and a gift to their children that could not be denied.

NuRtUrInG tHe LoVe Of SlEeP

Everyone in the family deserves and needs a good night's sleep. People are happier and more productive the next day if they've slept well. Some parents choose to sleep with their children until each decides to sleep by themself. Others yearn for the day when their child will fall asleep in their own room and bed. These parents hope, expect, or possibly fantasize that their child will go to bed at 8 o'clock and sleep nonstop until 7 in the morning. To put your child on the path to actualizing this bedtime dream come true, start by establishing a positive and pleasant bedtime routine.

Playing into your child's imagination

Parents can also play into the child's imaginative life as they send their child off to bed. One mom used this approach: "Oh, I hear your animals and dolls yawning and yawning, they're so tired. They're waiting for you. They can't fall asleep without you. They're eager to hear the bedtime story. We had better go upstairs, get your pajamas on, and get into bed for a story. Then you and your animals and dolls will all be able to fall asleep."

One child's bedtime routine

With a little boy named Jamie, the bedtime routine starts at 7 o'clock. Mom points out that the big hand on the clock is on 12 and the little hand on the 7, and asks Jamie to take a look: "What time is it Jamie?" He knows it's time to get ready for bed. Dad is the one who conducts this routine in the Frantz household. He likes it; it's one-on-one time with his son.

First comes a bath with bubbles, boats, and buoys. There's lots of chatter between father and son, plus giggles and splashing and time for imaginative play. Sometimes the bath alone takes 30 minutes. Now it's time for going potty, brushing teeth, putting on pj's and climbing into bed for as many stories as possible before the little hand on the clock reaches the 8.

Now it's time for a hug, a kiss, and a prayer, then lights out. Jamie needs his blanket for comfort and a night-light to see around his room and the way to the bathroom if he needs to go there.

At 4½ years old Jamie is not a napper so by the time his head hits the pillow, he's soon asleep. Jamie's well established bedtime routine sends him off to never-neverland where he's happy until the next morning. Like most people, he sometimes wakes in the middle of the night. When he does, he doesn't need Mom or Dad, because he has learned to put himself back to sleep.

Wow! Getting the kids in bed can work!

By establishing a positive bedtime routine and playing into your child's imagination, parents create positive associations with bedtime and sleep. Yelling at kids to get in their bed and go to sleep does not create these positive associations. In some homes children fight going to bed. They shed tears and throw tantrums and try more than once to rejoin Mom and Dad in front of the TV.

If you and your child are involved in a negative bedtime routine, you need to switch it into a positive one. This takes work, as children rely on the consistency of a routine even if it's a negative one. If your child makes three trips up and down the stairs—with tears and tantrums—before finally staying in his room and falling asleep, those trips, tears, and tantrums are part of the bedtime routine.

You can break this bedtime habit by offering the last kiss and hug and then sitting outside your child's door and saying every 5 minutes in monotone, "Mommy's (or Daddy's) here, it's time to go to sleep." Say exactly the same thing every time; your child will tire of your uninspiring and uninteresting line and fall asleep after only a bit of crying, complaining, or pleading. You've got fatigue working on your side.

Another approach is to lie down with your child until he falls asleep. Watch yourself; you may fall asleep sooner than your child. Lie down with your child for three to four nights until he falls asleep; then sit by your child, touching him for three to four nights; then sit by him not touching him for three to four nights; and finally move outside your child's door. You're gradually withdrawing your support as your child—in small steps—learns to stay in bed and settle himself to sleep.

Musical beds

In other homes a child might fall asleep without a problem but then wake up in the middle of the night. If he's not able to put himself back to sleep, he sneaks in bed with mommy and daddy.

Then dad might wake up from a little body fidgeting beside him, so he escorts his child back to bed and lies down with him until the child falls asleep. The two might feel crowded, so dad will venture back to sleep with his wife, but now the younger child is in his spot, so dad resorts to sleeping on the sofa. It's musical beds and everyone's just trying to find a place to sleep.

For those middle-of-the-night visits, the minute you realize your child is in your bed, escort him back to his bed. It's tough to do when you're groggy and don't expect that your child will stop—those visits are a habit, after all. However, if you keep putting your child back in his own bed, in time, he'll learn to stay in his bed and put himself back to sleep when he wakes up in the middle of the night. This is a skill all children need to learn; it's the parents' job to give their children the opportunity to do so.

Nightmares

Once your child is sleeping well she might wake up from a dream— sugar plums dancing in her head—or nightmares—a visit from the wicked witch of the North. Dreams and nightmares occur during the early morning hours when a person isn't in a deep sleep.

Children's minds hold memories of what has happened during the day. During the night they dream, but, because the line between fantasy and reality is so thin for young children, they don't understand that what they imagined only took place in their mind.

The mental picture might be scary, with monsters, goblins, and witches turning an imaginative adventure into a nightmare. Or the dream could be less frightening, involving dump trucks, cranes, and bulldozers working on a neighborhood road. But, both are perplexing and bewildering to the child.

When an adult wakes up from a dream or a nightmare, no matter how alarming or convoluted, he knows it didn't really occur. The adult clears his mind and goes back to sleep.

When a young child has a dream or a nightmare, it's tough for her to shake it on his own. Therefore, Mom or Dad needs to go into the bedroom and offer comfort and an explanation of what occurred:

"You had a nightmare (or a dream). It was scary. It seemed real but it wasn't. Your dream was pretend, it didn't really happen. I'll stay with you until you fall asleep."

Night terrors

Night terrors are altogether different. Typically, they terrify parents but not the child having them. Night terrors take place during the first few hours after a child falls asleep. Awakening from a deep sleep, the child will cry uncontrollably or will emit piercing screams; he can't be consoled. The child appears intensely fearful, yet in the morning he doesn't remember the event at all. Needless to say, the episode is disconcerting for parents.

Parents worry that something is physically or emotionally troubling their child and that the child's problem is manifesting itself in the middle of the night.

Children may have episodes of night terrors once a month or once a week, but the terrors are of no consequence to the children. If they occur every night it's best for the parent to consult with a sleep specialist.

The taming of a night terror

My twenty-seven-month-old was having night terrors; they occurred every couple of months, and didn't last very long. One night, though, she was hysterical for about an hour. Her eyes were open but she didn't acknowledge me or her daddy; she flailed about, attempting to hit and kick us, and she screamed at the top of her lungs and cried.

She does have a new sibling who is just over three months old. I have returned to work part time and she has begun preschool at a child-care center. I worry that all of these transitions could be triggering the terrors.

It is hard to comfort her without picking her up. I have always heard that you shouldn't try to wake up a child who is having a terror and that you shouldn't touch the child—the opposite of my instinct.

Since that hour-long night terror, we've established a consistent evening and bedtime routine. We've moved bedtime up an hour and miraculously she rarely has night terrors. When one does occur, we soothe her back to sleep by repeating this mantra for 5 to7 minutes: "You are safe. Mommy and Daddy love you. It is time to go night-night." She no longer thrashes about, but she does sit up, eyes wide open, and moves her arms in an odd way, as if she is crawling or swimming. After hearing the mantra, she lays right down and falls asleep. All of these episodes happen 1 to 2 hours after going to bed.

LeArN tO lOvE tHe PoTtY

Teaching children to use the toilet today is far different than in generations past. Your grandmother is likely to question you by saying, "When in the world are you going to train that child of yours to use the potty?" In Grandma's day it was her accomplishment, but today it's the child's. Besides, with disposable diapers and many people involved in teaching the child—Mom, Dad, Grandma, and child-care provider—not to mention busy family schedules, it often takes the child longer to get out of the habit of using diapers. Now this occurs somewhere between two and three years old, yet some children don't master the skill until three and a half years old.

Although learning to use the toilet is something the child controls—it's his body, not yours—there's much that parents can do to guide the child to success. Most important, let the child know that although he will learn in his own way and time, someday he will learn to use the toilet like everyone else. Parents need to set aside time to guide the child to use the toilet with consistency, not force.

Preparing

- When your child is eighteen months old, buy a potty chair and place it in the bathroom. When your child sits on it, take notice, establish eye contact, and say, "Look at you, you're sitting on the potty just like Mommy and Daddy."
- If you have a little potty that sits on the floor, to familiarize your child with toileting, bring the potty chair out of the bathroom. Your child can sit on it when watching TV. Put dolls and Teddy bear on it, too.
- Establish the routine of having your child sit on the potty before climbing into the bathtub and before putting on his pajamas. Don't expect your child to actually use the potty at this point. This is just to get your child familiar with sitting on the toilet.
- Encourage your child to come into the bathroom with you. He can hand you toilet paper, and when you're finished, he can flush the toilet. You lose your privacy but take heart, it doesn't last forever.
- Have your child set his teddy bear on the toilet and play through a toileting scenario with the teddy peeing or pooping, wiping, flushing, and then pretending to wash his paws.

Getting started

- Once your child turns two, notice if your child is dry for up to 1½ hours and stops playing or walking to poop. These are signs of control; it's time to start teaching your child to use the toilet part time.
- Put your child in light cotton underwear for a 2-hour period every day. You can put a rubber pant or a disposable training pant over the panties. Then, after the first hour of this 2-hour period take your child to use the toilet. Don't ask your child, "Do you want to sit on the potty?" Any two-year-old will automatically say "No!" Just say, "It's time to sit on the potty." Once your child is on the toilet, encourage him to go but don't show disappointment if he doesn't perform. Validate the importance of practicing which is a very important step on the road to potty training.

- Once your child starts performing on the toilet, have him wear underwear at home. Use a disposable training pant or cloth panties with a rubber pant over them when going to the grocery store or Grandma's.
- Soon you'll be brave enough to put your child in underwear full-time.
- Be sure to consult with your child-care provider about how she proceeds with toilet training. Usually experienced caregivers are skilled at teaching children to use the toilet. Working together and communicating is key to your child's progress.
- Be prepared to deal with accidents. Don't be horrified when a child poops or pees in his panties. Clean the child and the floor with a matter-of-fact attitude. Then put him on the toilet so the child will eventually make the connection that urine and stool go in the toilet.

Resistance

- Some children meet with no success. The task becomes frustrating for both parent and child. If this occurs with your child, keep the child in disposable training pants but take a break from any rigorous training. Wait a couple of months and then try again. Often the gift of time is all the child needs.
- If potty training becomes an emotional battle over who is in control, drop back and give it a rest. Adjust your frame of mind by realizing that ultimate control lies with the child; it's his body, not yours. After a break of a month or so, try introducing the potty again.
- Your role in the potty training process is to positively influence your child to use the toilet when the child's body is physically developed to the point where he can hold in the urine and stool, and then release it into

the toilet. It's important to remain upbeat while verbalizing that the child will, in his own way and time, learn to use the toilet. Do all you can to avoid coercing, forcing, or manipulating your child to use the toilet.

- If you find yourself in a potty training power struggle tell your child this: "Your job is to learn to use the toilet, my job is to help you learn. It's your body. Someday you'll pee and poop in the toilet. If you want to wear underpants, that's fine. If you want to wear training pants, that's fine, too. You decide. When you want to use the toilet is up to you. I'll help you."

- If your child becomes constipated, retains bowel movements, or develops encopresis (involuntary passage of bowel often as a result of constipation), seek medical help. If your child is approaching four years old and continues to have numerous wetting accidents, talk to your doctor.

Night trainInG

Once your child begins to use the toilet with ease, you'll wonder when your child will stay dry through the night. A few children learn simultaneously to use the toilet during the day and stay dry all through the night. These children are rare. If your child is not like this, don't worry; most children stay dry through the night about six months after they're fully accustomed to using the toilet during daytime hours.

When you realize that your child's diaper is dry more mornings than it is wet, suggest to your child to try going to sleep without a diaper or disposable training pant. With a diaper on, it gives the child license to pee. Without a diaper many children will catch on, staying dry all night long, every night.

Incentives

If you believe your child can stay dry but he doesn't, think about an incentive chart. Try this approach for children over five years old. When your child wakes up dry, place a sticker on the chart. After five dry nights—not necessarily consecutive—give the child a reward: maybe a new Lego set, a dollar bill, or a pack of Pokémon cards. When your child remains dry night after night, week after week, the chart is no longer needed. Don't worry, he won't go back to wetting his bed, he's developed the habit of staying dry all night long.

If, despite the chart, your child continues to wet the bed—producing only frustration and feelings of failure—end the incentive plan. Even the most inspiring incentive can't prompt a child to do something his body, because of delayed maturation, can't do.

real life parenting

Jason's story

Four-year-old Jason woke up every morning with a soaked diaper. As Mom diapered him before bedtime one evening, she found herself saying, "Jason, I'd like you to try tonight to stay dry and to sleep without a diaper." Lo and behold, the next morning Jason was dry! With his diaper on he peed freely. With it off, he was more aware of his bodily sensations and therefore was able to stay dry all night long.

Another interesting note about Jason: When school began each fall, he had bed-wetting accidents. This phenomenon lasted until third grade. Why? Because the change from summertime to school-time schedule and adjusting to the new school year were stressful occasions for him.

Any childhood stress—a new sibling, moving, parents' divorce—can trigger bed wetting. Usually it takes about a month until the child returns to dry nights. If this situation occurs with your child, manage it with patience and kindness. Exasperation on your part only exacerbates things.

Children who wet the bed

The bedwetting statistics are as follows: 10 percent of five-year-olds and 5 percent of ten-years-olds wet the bed. Behind every child who experiences enuresis (involuntary bed-wetting), there's usually a family member who did the same: Bedwetting is hereditary. Some children inherit their small bladders while others inherit the propensity to sleep though everything, including the sensation of needing to urinate.

So what's a parent to do? Let's say your eight-year-old pees in his bed every night. Every morning you face laundry that needs washing. To complicate the issue, your child has been invited to spend the night with friends, which you haven't allowed in a loving attempt to protect your child from the embarrassment of wet pajamas and sheets at a friend's home.

First, eliminate as much laundry as possible. Put a plastic sheet on the mattress. Go ahead and put a bedspread or comforter on your child's bed, but when you put him to bed at night take it off his bed and replace it with a slumber bag (a sleeping bag that's made for indoor rather than outdoor sleeping). In the morning when the child gets up he can put his pajamas and the slumber bag in the washing machine. It might be a good idea to have an additional bag on hand just in case you aren't able to wash that slumber bag every day.

The point is to manage the situation rather than be exasperated by it daily. It serves no purpose to talk each morning about the wet bed trying to convince and ultimately pressure the child to do something his body is not yet ready to do.

Offer an explanation

If your child wets the bed, it's probably best to explain to him why he wets the bed even though his friends or siblings don't. "You know, children's bodies develop differently. Some children, like you, learn to read at six years old; others don't learn until they're eight. Some children stay dry all night at three; for others, it just takes longer."

When a child who wets the bed spends the night with a friend

Here's what Shannon did. She would call the hosting parent and in a forthright fashion explain her child's inclination to wet the bed. She said, "Sometimes Collin wets the bed. When he comes to spend the night at your house, he'll bring a sleeping bag and sleep on the floor. In the morning if he's wet, he'll take care of his wet pajamas and sleeping bag. It's not a problem for him; I hope it isn't a problem for you."

In time, Collin gained control of urinating in the middle of the night, and his self-esteem didn't suffer because his parents understood his inadvertent tendency to wet the bed. Today, he's a stockbroker, married and with a baby of his own. His parents' attitude of acceptance along with teaching their son how to manage the situation protected him from embarrassment that another approach might have caused.

Don't Be Scared of the baby tooth!

You'll hear it from your dentist, "Once that first little tooth emerges from a child's gum it's important to clean it." No need to panic. It's not necessary to scrub it with a toothbrush and toothpaste; you only need to brush it lightly with a wet baby-sized toothbrush or even simply wipe it clean with a damp cloth. Whichever method works, your dentist will likely insist that you—the parent—need to do all you can to keep that baby tooth germ-free.

While cleaning your child's teeth is important for dental hygiene, it's also important to teach your child how to brush teeth to establish good dental habits. You clean your child's teeth today with the goal that in time he'll take pride in his clean teeth and eventually take responsibility for the task of brushing and flossing all on his own.

You thought cleaning teeth was simple?

If you're too insistent and too intrusive, your well-meaning intentions for clean teeth could backfire. An emotional battle of wills could break out between you and your child over an event that should be as much a part of a child's day as sleeping, eating, and going to the potty.

To adults, brushing teeth is a habit. Although you're aware that there are several steps to the process, they are so automatic that it seems like one simple task. To a child, however, each step in the teeth brushing process stands alone, and he doesn't automatically see that one step is connected to the next. And besides, young children get easily distracted. Water flowing out of the faucet magically turns into a waterfall with fairies swimming in the pool of water. The child isn't dawdling; he's in an imaginary world of his own. That's why he needs a parent to see that the task is completed, while gradually withdrawing support until the child is an independent teeth brusher.

The 14 steps to clean teeth

The child:

1. Walks into the bathroom.
2. Climbs up on a stool.
3. Locates the toothbrush and toothpaste.
4. Puts the toothpaste on the toothbrush.
5. Wets the toothbrush.
6. Brushes the teeth, first alone, then with help from the parent.
7. Rinses the teeth with water.
8. Spits the water into the sink.
9. Wipes the mouth with a towel.
10. Smiles in the mirror to see how nice the teeth look.
11. Feels the teeth with the tongue to see how nice and clean they feel.
12. Puts away the toothpaste and toothbrush.
13. Climbs down from the stool.
14. Walks out of the bathroom.

Can you believe it? There are 14 steps to this one little task.

Copycat learning

It helps if the parent and child brush their teeth at the same time. (And you thought you couldn't multi-task!) When you stand at the sink together, your child, who learns most efficiently by mimicking you, catches on to the process more quickly. It's best to teach one or two steps at a time and keep your eyes on your child as he brushes his teeth. Also, praise him as he takes on a new step as his own.

Don't raise your expectations too high, as it takes some children until they're eight years old before they are thorough and independent teeth brushers. The parent's role starts by doing all of the steps for the child until he can do it on his own and then the parent only has to remind and monitor the process.

real life parenting

Ending a teeth brushing power struggle

Emma, age six, and her mom were in a teeth brushing power struggle. Her mom would nag, threaten, plead, and scold Emma each night to brush her teeth. Emma would whine and pout before finally making a feeble attempt. Finally, her mom decided to invest in a few tubes of differently flavored toothpaste: bubble gum, vanilla mint, cinnamon, and peppermint.

Then they played the toothpaste guessing game. Emma would go into the bathroom, pick a flavor, brush her teeth, and then blow her breath on Mom. Mom then guessed which flavor Emma had used. By the time the toothpaste game had run its course, Emma had become an independent and competent tooth brusher, sometimes playing the toothpaste game with Grandma or others who dropped by for a visit.

You can be clever, too, just like Emma's mom, by creating a fun game and leaving frustrations behind.

The dReAded WoRd "ChOrEs"

Children should do chores. Why? Because kids make messes, so they need to clean them up. Kids get clothes dirty, so they need to toss them in the laundry. And kids eat and use dishes, so they need to help in the kitchen.

When kids are two-years-old they like to help. They want to fold socks, stir the pancake batter, and empty the dishwasher. They want to do what you do and, of course, most of their help isn't help at all.

Despite this, let them help out as best they can. Go overboard to compliment them, smile, and show your approval. Let them know what good helpers they are—it will pay off in the long run.

Do chores together until your child is five. Put toys away with your preschooler. Be specific about what needs to be done, "The blocks go in this container. Let's do it together; it will go faster."

Then when they're five, let them choose a chore that is theirs. It could be feeding the dog, setting or clearing the table, or emptying the garbage. Any of these are good because you're around to coach and cheer them on.

Make the job clear. Show them how you want the task done, teach them in small steps, and don't expect perfection. Remember, they're only five. Realize, too, that for years they'll continue to need friendly one-word reminders: "garbage," "dog," or "dishes."

Establish a deadline. For young children, an event may be better than a specific time. "The table needs to be set before you can watch your favorite TV show."

Praise the child. Talk up and praise their efforts. "What a good job, thank you. It's so much fun having you in the kitchen helping. I enjoy having you here with me." Offer praise and appreciation particularly until the chore becomes a habit, but at the same time be insistent about what you expect.

Use "when". "*When* the dishes are dried, you can play a video game." "*When* the toys are put away, you can go outside." "When" is positive and says it will happen, sooner or later.

Watch your tone of voice. Be firm and kind. A child may gripe and whine but nevertheless insist that the job gets done. Use this line, "You can cry and complain all you want. And when you're done crying and complaining, you'll need to set the table."

Use chore force—similar to centrifugal force

As children get older, increase the number of chores they are responsible for but don't overwhelm them—they still need time for play and homework.

Some parents are extremely skilled at inspiring their kids to do their chores. It's a force similar to gravity—no one really likes it or questions it, it just happens and we all learn to live with it. It's a force similar to gravity—no one really questions it, it just happens and all learn to live with it. It takes the most work with the oldest child, but once chore life is established, the task of teaching children to pitch in gets easier. Try the line, "In this family, everyone helps out!" Consistency is essential.

Chore force in action

Here are some examples of setting chores:
- No one leaves the kitchen after dinner until the dishes are done: Everyone helps—that's the way it is. Each child questions this rule at some point but the parents win out.
- No one leaves the house each day until beds are made and clothes are hung up or put in the dirty clothes hamper.
- No one goes out to play or to soccer practice on Saturday morning until bedrooms and bathrooms are tidy.

The parents' discipline and insistence are admirable and essential to success. It's not being mean and pushy; it's just something everyone does together.

How to make chores work

One Mom used chore-force to pull her kids into the kitchen to help with dinner. It's just something they all did together in the evening. This has really this paid off for her. She works full-time now that her boys are in junior high and high school. On Saturday morning they each—Dad and Mom, too—choose a menu and a night they'll be available to cook.

Three nights a week Mom walks in from work to the smells of tacos, chili, or spaghetti. Don't you envy her? And think of the skills these boys will have to survive on their own. They won't have to rely on fast foods or frozen dinners.

Even if your children end up becoming princes or princesses, and never ever have to clean a toilet again after leaving home, they will still benefit from the discipline you instilled from insisting they do chores.

I fEeL sTuPiD aSkInG, bUt HoW mUcH sHoUlD i FeEd My ChIlD?

I know. You feel a bit dumb, why? Because you have no idea how much you should feed your child. But don't worry—you can't automatically know this.

Parents of toddlers and preschoolers often wonder if their children are eating enough. Toddlers eat less than infants mainly because they're not growing as fast. Preschool-aged children eat more but they certainly don't eat adult-sized portions.

If you're concerned about your child's eating habits, before panicking and making an unnecessary appointment with a nutritionist, ask yourself the following:

"Is my child healthy, sleeping well, energetic, and growing?"

If he is, he's probably getting the food and nutrition he needs. If he isn't, then it's time to call your pediatrician who might then refer you to a nutritionist.

Most toddlers and preschoolers are picky eaters. If you have the expectation that your youngster will eat three meals a day and a wide variety of foods, get rid of that notion right away. Young children like the same foods over and over again and usually do best on five small meals a day.

Toddlers

During some meals, toddlers eat. More often, they take only a few bites and sometimes they dump most of it on the floor. Realize that much of the time eating to them is a sensory, scientific, and psychological experience.

Sensory experience
Because children learn by using all their senses, they not only see, smell, and taste food but learn about it by touching it and smearing it on their high chair, hands, and face and by listening to the sounds it makes in and out of their mouths.

Scientific experience
Toddlers are little scientists; they're interested in gravity and how different food items splat on the floor—juice pours from a cup differently than milk and macaroni lands differently than yogurt. So rather than an experience in eating, mealtime becomes a scientific experiment.

Psychological experience
And because you might react to such eating antics with frustration, exasperation, or horror, your child, being the little psychologist that he is—trying to understand human behavior and emotions—is eager to watch your responses as he learns about gravity. "Huh, that's interesting, when I drop macaroni he looks perplexed. When I deliberately spill my milk he's angry. Well, let's see how he responds when I dump my plate on the floor."

Do your best to keep your antagonism to a minimum and progress through the toddler months by setting mealtime routines, but once your child starts playing with or dropping food, get his down from his high chair.

Toddlers are often out to prove they have a mind of their own, so if your toddler realizes that eating certain foods are very important to you, he'll probably approach these foods with a closed-mouth attitude.

The food rules of toddlerdom

Hold on to the goal that your child will eat a broad selection of nutritious foods, but realize that how your child eats during the challenging two-year-old period has little to do with how he'll eat in the future.

Rule No. 1: Realize that most toddlers like the same foods day in and day out.

Rule No. 2: Keep in mind that toddlers who nurse or drink milk from a bottle eat less solid food.

Rule No. 3: Resist coaxing, coercing, or enticing your toddler to eat his meals.

Rule No. 4: Give positive attention for the food he does eat. Say, "You ate some rice. Yummy, it's good. I'll eat my rice, too."

Rule No. 5: Prompt your toddler along by saying, "I saw you eat all your applesauce. Now try a piece of cheese."

Rule No. 6: Prepare yourself for the inevitable, "No! Icky cheese!" with his head turned away.

Rule No. 7: Respond with, "Oh, you don't care for cheese today? Maybe you'll eat it another day."

Rule No. 8: After you've eaten your bite of cheese, describe its delicious taste: "I just love cheddar cheese; it's so yummy." Notice if your child copies your eating ways.

As children grow

- Avoid being a short order cook. Each mealtime, put out some foods you know your children will eat and other new foods that you hope they'll eventually try and savor.
- Don't engage in an eating battle of wills. If you find yourself in one, drop out. Some eating power plays carry on for years; this is a path you want to avoid.
- Establish this rule at your house: Make a meal with the food on the table. This means that parents put the food on the table and the children decide what they will put on their plates and what they will swallow.
- Make every meal relaxed and conversational. Focus on your children by talking about what they did during that day, or what they'll be doing later.
- Sit with your children during breakfast, lunch, and dinner.
- Teach your children about nutrition. With childhood obesity being such a concern these days, and the advertising of fast food and snacks so widespread in the media, it's best for parents to stand their ground against such foods from early on. Declare your family's position of healthful eating and hold to it.
- Say "no" to fast foods and junk food. Establish a family-eating slogan such as, "Our family doesn't eat junk because we are not junk." "We don't eat fatty foods because we don't want to be fat like those foods."
- Allow children to snack on fruit, veggies, low fat cheese, and nutritious crackers between meals.
- Rely on the fact that children are great imitators and parents are powerful role models. Gradually—between three and eight years old—they'll be eating what you eat.
- Allow tweens and teens who are voracious eaters to eat when they're hungry. Do all you can to make sure that the foods you provide are nutritious and healthy.

real life parenting

Alan's case

Between the ages of eighteen months and five years Alan's diet consisted mostly of homemade chicken noodle soup and macaroni and cheese. By the time he was eight years old, he was eating sushi.

Long live the family meal!

It seems that family dinners are falling by the wayside. Frequently, both parents are working to varying schedules, while the children are involved in extracurricular activities, and the TV is an irresistible distraction. This all results in the traditional evening meal occurring once a week rather then once a day in many families.

Some families find that breakfast is the meal where they all gather around the table, not only for eating but also for conversation and enjoying each others' company.

Regardless of when this meal occurs, it's important. It's a solidification of the family unit whether you're Lisa and Emma (a single mom and her daughter), who eat their evening meal at Grandma's, or the Dykes who have 11 children and who never know exactly how many of their children, ages six to twenty-six, will show up for a meal.

Family meals don't need to be rigidly adhered to. But try to find time when you can all sit down together and talk. It's an important bonding experience.

Do you dare take your child out to eat?

Let's say you're considering taking your eight-year-old to a restaurant: you realize there's a problem at hand. She doesn't know to put her napkin on her lap, her elbows rest on the table, and she talks with food in her mouth. Oops. It seems you've neglected manners instructions.

Home dining today is definitely less formal than in past generations, and that's not all bad, but in any civilized society there's a code of conduct everyone must learn, like it or not. It means you can get through your meal without wincing in embarrassment. For children to learn table manners, they're required to appreciate a fairly complicated set of skills that may take years to master. Don't just hope your kids catch on—it isn't that simple.

For families who eat casually or on the go, it's harder to educate kids for family dinners and dining out. But kids need to learn to sit at the table without getting up and down at will, and to properly use a knife, fork, and spoon.

Think about the table manners that are important to you, and be conscious of teaching these in a deliberate, intentional manner. There's no need to make dinner a setting for strict manners instruction, however. With a relaxed atmosphere, children are usually quite receptive to etiquette instruction.

You, too, can teach good manners!

- Instruct in small portions. Use a step-by-step fashion, working on one or two manners at a time.
- Use a variety of approaches. Show your child how to put his napkin on his lap. Give a one-word reminder: "napkin" is all you need to say. Offer a nonverbal cue by just pointing to the napkin.
- Stay consistent. Every time your son comes to the table with his baseball cap on, remind him politely to remove it: "No hats at the table, please."
- Model good manners. You can even point them out to your children. "I always serve my guests first; it's a polite gesture, honoring the guest." Conversely, if you talk when your mouth is full of food, the likelihood is great your kids will do the same.
- Declare what you expect from your children. On your way to Aunt Betty's, explain: "If Auntie serves a dish you don't care to eat, just pass it along or say, 'I don't care for sweet potatoes, thank you Auntie.'"
- Be complimentary. "I heard you say 'please pass the gravy,' that was thoughtful and polite."
- Don't expect perfection. If you're a perfectionist in the courtesy category you might be setting yourself up for a manners war. If one starts to erupt, remain a good model but back off. Your child holds the controls in this power struggle.

Young children refer to you for what to do in social situations, and later they turn to their peers. Now that's a frightening thought. That's why it's so important to teach the habits of courteous behavior when children are preschoolers, and keep them up at home. Don't be surprised when the manners you've worked hard to instill are temporarily forgotten when your children are teens.

Teenagers—dinner table turned battlefield

No matter how skilled and consistent you are at instilling manners, some teens deliberately reject your education in etiquette. Despite this dismissal, keep it. Explain the conventional approach. Maybe your teenage daughter won't change her behavior now, but someday when she's a bank executive and lunching with the bank president, she'll retrieve your manners curriculum that has been hibernating for years.

The key to teaching children courteous conduct is to do it without embarrassment or disrespect. If your child is talking while chewing, it's okay to ask him to swallow first and then talk, but it's not okay to do this when your teenage son's new girlfriend is dining with the family for the first time.

Explain to your children that rules of etiquette are important not simply as codes to live by, but as acts of consideration for others.

De-stressing two difficult daily transitions

Two of the most difficult habits to establish in any household are the "getting out the door" in the morning and the "coming back home" in the evening routines.

In the morning there's typically a beat-the-clock syndrome as parents and children fight to get to work and school on time. In some households there are tears and tantrums each day from either parent or child, or both, as parents prod and children resist doing what's necessary to make it out the door on time.

The time that everyone reconvenes later in the day can sometimes be another stressful transition. Making it over the threshold and shifting into the evening schedule can involve a release of emotion and stress that has built up throughout the day.

It is worthwhile, therefore, to create a twice-a-day habit of de-stressing for your family.

De-stressing in the morning

De-stress before family members disperse for their day and again when returning home. You might read a story to your child each morning, sing a song together, or pretend you're wet puppies and shake like crazy to release the stress that's building in your bodies as you all anticipate leaving the house and embarking on your day.

You may simply breathe deeply while playing soothing music. None of these activities takes very long—3 to 5 minutes—but when you engage in any of these calming activities everyone leaves home with a feeling of well-being rather than one of stress.

Once the stress is gone, remind children to head to the bathroom for potty time and teeth brushing and then guide them as they locate their shoes, coats, and backpacks.

De-stressing in the evening

It isn't unusual for children to turn clingy or, worse yet, have a meltdown when they get back together with their parents at the end of the day. It's release after good behavior. All day kids do their best to manage themselves as best they can. Once home they feel the need to let down or let loose.

Parents aren't that different. When returning from work they need a little time to themselves. Without it they may explode, cry, or hide in the bathroom or behind the newspaper. Such a push–pull between parents and children might routinely end up in turmoil.

To avoid the tears and family uproar when the family reconvenes, it's important for parents to immediately make themselves available to their children. Cross the threshold, put everything down, grab a simple snack from the refrigerator, put on some soothing music, and sit down.

Depending on your parenting style and the age of your children, you might play, talk, cuddle, sing, dance, read, or wrestle with them.

These de-stressing activities offer your children the positive attention they're seeking. That's what they need and want; it only takes 5 to 10 minutes. Once they're comforted from contact with Mom or Dad, then it's the parents' turn to read the mail and scan the newspaper for 15 to 20 minutes. Once relaxed, it's time to start a simple supper, often with the children involved.

A brief relaxation activity before school and work prepares you and your children emotionally and mentally for learning and being productive. A relaxing after-school and after-work ritual releases the stress-filled episodes that children and parents may have experienced during the day.

By establishing a stress-reducing ritual before and after school, parents not only provide everyone with better mental and physical health, but children carry this habit with them through the tween and teen years when they no longer have Mom or Dad leading the activity.

CHAPTER 5

BETTER

BEHAVIOR

Take The lEaD— pRoAcTiVe PaReNtInG

No parent wants to be a pushover. Although you might find yourself in that position from time to time, you hope that as a parent you've got a handle on how to guide your children to better behavior—not just for your sake, but theirs, too. It's best to start with a proactive approach. You do so by building up a reservoir of positive interactions that tell your children that you love them. This reservoir is critical because when your children misbehave and you correct their behavior, they'll more likely remedy their ways because deep in their hearts they sense that you've got their best interest in mind. They'll truly want to live up to your expectations for better behavior.

And then on a day when you blow it, say things you don't mean, and are too harsh or punishing, your relationship will recover quickly because of the huge positive reservoir of love and trust you've built up between you and your child.

Five proactive parenting approaches

If you're a parent who nags, yells, or gets frustrated with children who don't behave, it's time to incorporate these five proactive approaches into your parenting repertoire. By using them daily, without ever using any more hard-and-fast disciplinary techniques, your children's behavior will instantly improve, guaranteed! Give at least one a try today. By doing so, you'll instantly experience more joy in parenting.

Proactive parenting approach #1

Child leads the play: 15 minutes a day, no strings attached

Say to your two to ten-year-old child:

"For the next 15 minutes, we're going to spend time together. What we do is up to you. You're the boss."

Does the thought of putting your child in charge scare you? If you can set your parenting fears aside for just 15 minutes a day and let your child be the boss, you'll be using the first approach in your proactive parenting repertoire.

Parents might worry that their child would then choose to color on walls or eat junk food nonstop for the entire 15 minutes. It's unlikely. Usually children choose building with blocks, creating with art materials, or playing a game.

Let's say your child decides to build a tower with blocks. Once he begins, then you construct a tower, too. You might be tempted to make yours more elaborate, but don't. Just make your building resemble your child's. By imitating your child's tower, you flatter him; he's then inspired to build more.

If your child chooses a game to play, let your child determine the rules even if they're not what the game creators intended. If it's artwork, copy your child's picture and do what he does with markers, glue, scissors, tape, and paper.

As the playtime progresses, let your child lead the conversation. Avoid giving commands or asking questions. If the child says, "It's a house," all you say is, "Oh, I see you made a house." You can add, "I'm building one like yours."

If you feel the need to talk more, provide a play-by-play account of your child's appropriate behavior—for example, "I see you put the red block on top of the blue block." Your child actually takes your description as a compliment, not only reinforcing but prolonging her positive behavior.

There is one more added bonus for you: As you watch and describe your child taking control of this play situation, you're likely to see her with new eyes as the competent person she is. Then you'll find that this "letting your child lead an activity" will spill over into other parts of the day. You'll be more willing to let your child take charge while you step back, watch, and describe. Your child's competent behavior mushrooms, and the ripple effect is in place.

Tip: Children are expected to follow parents' rules, guidelines, and agenda most of the day. The miraculous aspect of the "15-minute child-led play time activity" is that when it's over and you say, "Now it's time for bath and bed," your child will be much more willing to comply.

Proactive parenting approach #2
Affirmation

No matter what their age, children really need affirmation. A child who isn't affirmed is left with a feeling of wanting. What is she wanting? Recognition—first for who she is and second for what she does.

If you're good at affirming your children, pat yourself on the back. If you're not sure, read on! Affirming children is a skill any parent can acquire and it's the second approach in proactive parenting.

Your baby just learned to make a sound using her fist and mouth. She makes the sound; you make it back with your fist in your mouth. She makes the sound again; you do the same again and again, copying her each time. Copying what she can do affirms her newly acquired skill.

Your toddler wants to play with a jack-in-the box. You turn the crank and watch the jack pop out. Your toddler is surprised, so you show surprise, too. You put jack back in the box and turn the crank again. You do so until the child tires of the game. It may take 17 times. But by repeating the play, you affirm the child's interest in objects disappearing and reappearing.

Your preschool-age child says, "I don't like playing with Lucy today. Send her home." Instead of scolding the child about the importance of being a good friend, you affirm her by saying, "It doesn't sound like you and Lucy are having fun. Come in the kitchen, I'll get out the play dough." Your affirming response saved the play date.

Your school-age child bounds in the door after school and drops her backpack and coat on the floor as she heads for the refrigerator. All the while she's excitedly telling you of her feats at soccer practice that day. "My team won at practice today. I scored three goals."

How does the parent affirm the child? By saying, "Good for you! What was the score?" Then a minute or two later, offer the reminder, "Don't forget to hang up your coat and put your backpack by the door ready for tomorrow."

A teenager offers this piece of information, "You know my friend, Jeremy? His dad bought him a new car." There is no need to say, "Well,

Jeremy's parents can afford it. We can't." Instead, make an affirming response, such as, "What kind of car did he buy?" That's all it takes to affirm your child's interest in his friend's newly acquired vehicle.

If you need to offer a reality check about the feasibility and affordability of buying a car for your teen, your information will be better received after the affirmation.

The affirmed child feels confident, self-assured, loved, and naturally works toward better behavior. The child who doesn't receive supportive affirmation looks for approval, as she doesn't know where she stands. The affirmed child, in time, learns to affirm herself, no longer needing it from her parents.

Proactive parenting approach #3
The gradual turning over of power and control

Wouldn't it be great if children were perfectly compliant until they moved out of the house? Unfortunately that's not how it is. As children travel the developmental years, they seek to grasp, bit-by-bit, more control of their lives.

Parenting is a gradual turnover of power and control from the parent to child. When parents determine just how to do it, they're using the third proactive parenting approach.

At about eighteen months, children discover they have a mind of their own and go overboard daily to prove it. The eight to ten-year-old age span are the "turnover" years. This is when the shift of power from the parent to the child reaches the halfway mark. For some parents and children this shift is gradual and graceful. For others, it involves lots of power struggles over who is in charge, parent or child.

The teen years bring about a whole new set of power surges. Teens want to be in control of themselves but they don't have the experience, judgment, or emotional stability to be completely independent. Conflict can occur on a daily basis.

The best way to sidestep power plays while slowly turning power and control over to children is to offer them choices and decision-making abilities appropriate to their age without jeopardizing their safety or your family's values.

Once preschool-aged, a child can choose which toys to play with, picture to draw, food to eat, and clothes to wear. School-age children decide between soccer and the swim team, ballet and gymnastics. They also want to have some choice about how to spend their allowance and how to arrange their bedrooms. Tweens and teens choose how to spend their leisure time and with whom, whether to take algebra or geometry, French or Spanish. They choose whether to get a job or not and even begin exploring options for their future.

By allowing this gradual turnover of power and control, your child will feel competent and that she's in control. Better behavior will follow!

Caution: Two-year-olds don't understand choices. If you ask a toddler if he wants pancakes or waffles for breakfast, he'll want both. So avoid offering toddlers choices, but when it seems okay, go along with their demands for the blue cup, the red chair, or the same pajamas night after night.

Proactive parenting approach #4

What does a gentle touch do?

Touch is the fourth technique in proactive parenting. Three things happen when parents gently touch their children:

1. Touch communicates unconditional love and acceptance without saying a word.

2. Touch is a control device for discipline: "I'll gently hold you to keep you from hurting others. I'm not going to allow you to pinch (scratch, or punch) but I'm not going to reject you, either. I'll control you until you can control yourself."

3. Gentle touch, massage, and loving strokes help bring a child's out-of-control body into control. If a baby's flailing around in his crib, crying, and out of control, of course you'd immediately pick up the baby, hold him close, rock him, and stroke his back until he's calm. Parents can use gentle touch as children get older, too.

All children get that frazzled out-of-control feeling; touch helps them regain control. And some children just need more hugs, pats, and cuddles than others.

Of course, sometimes children resist touch. When they're angry, they stomp away and want to be alone. Respect this but keep listening. As the child's wails turn to whimpers, that's your signal to draw your child onto your lap for holding and rocking.

You can't force a child to be touched. But parents, challenge yourselves to find the right moment when your child is receptive to holding, massage, or pats. Children need it just as they need food, sleep, exercise, and a stimulating environment.

The children who are most reluctant to receive touch are adolescents. They stand away, move off, and resist most kinds of physical contact with parents. Obviously your lanky teen won't fit on your lap, so try just sitting next to him as you watch TV, then move in behind and massage those shoulders or scratch that back.

And the bonus for all these hugs comes when you've had a lousy day, you feel frazzled and out of control, and your child just naturally sees your need for a hug and can give it spontaneously with ease.

real life parenting

The power of touch

Ciera is an eighteen-month-old who packs a mighty pinch. Four-year-old sister Brittany is her most frequent victim. Ciera's pinch is so vicious it sometimes it leaves bruises and draws blood.

Instead of sending Ciera to her room for an isolated time out, when Ciera pinches, Mom gently moves toward Ciera, bends down, softly surrounds Ciera with her arms. She massages her hands and fingers while saying, "No, pinching. Pat your sister." And then she demonstrates how to pat lovingly. Ciera's tense body relaxes as she sits on her mother's lap.

Miraculously, after about three more pinching and massaging episodes, the pinching drops out of sight. This is the power of touch, and most parents don't use it enough. If for some reason the technique isn't effective, it may be necessary to consult a behavior specialist.

Proactive parenting approach #5

Quality time

Quality time is reading the same story over and over because your toddler insists. It's letting your preschooler help make a pie even when your in-laws are coming for dinner. It's pulling yourself away from watching a televised baseball game to fix your child's swing.

Quality time is now. It's taking time away from your agenda to focus on your children's. It means turning off the TV even when kids protest about it.

One full-time working mom, after picking up her daughter at child care, would go grocery shopping. Sound exhausting? Not to this Mom. She makes grocery shopping part of their quality time by including her child in selecting food, and talking about prices and the importance of good nutrition.

Quality time, however, is not just those blissful times of parenting. It's being up at 3:00 A.M. giving a cool bath to your baby who has a 104-degree temperature. It's taking vacation time to attend school programs and conferences. It's standing on the sidelines on a cold wet Saturday morning watching your child play soccer.

Quality time is allowing your twelve-year-old daughter to have a slumber party, thereby giving up your sleep and sanity for 24 hours. It's being with that same daughter at fifteen when she has just experienced her first break-up with a boy. At this time you probably don't have the words to comfort and soothe her, so you just hold her and cry together.

Quality time is when you get a call from the police saying your son was caught stealing a video game. You leave your job to face the situation; you don't know how to handle this one but you know your presence alone will have impact.

Let's start to think of quality parenting rather than quality time. This involves the full range of your parenting responsibility.

You can be a quality parent even though you're busy. The key is to know when to step in and get involved with the necessary and sometimes messy, time-consuming parts of being a parent and when it's time to back off.

This level of quality that parents seek involves occasionally setting your needs aside for the needs of your children. It's giving up of yourself for your kids, but it doesn't mean giving up your life. The key is to know when to put your needs aside.

> **Being a quality parent involves making a mental check list:**
> ❑ Have I held my toddler today?
> ❑ Have I taken time to focus on each child?
> ❑ Did I concentrate when my ten-year-old related the details of his baseball game?
> ❑ Did I listen when my teenager gossiped about her girlfriend?

When children have troubles with school or friends, parents want them to talk about it so they can console and counsel their children. But without a solid relationship base that says, "I'm available and I'm here," the children won't come for those crucial moments when you really need to be involved.

Quality parenting often involves knowing when to seek professional advice to make it through the rigors of parenting with dignity.

But without question there cannot be quality parenting without a certain quantity of the most precious commodities you possess: Time and positive, focused attention.

Being a quality parent has a lot to do with seizing opportunities to clear your mind so that you can concentrate on your child to assure her she's important.

Now that you're acquainted with these approaches to proactive parenting, you're ready to take on methods and techniques for handling childrens' misbehaviors.

Why can't my children be born good?

Why don't children automatically comply? It's mainly because each has a mind of his own. Ultimately each wants to be under his own power and control rather than yours. So the dilemma for parents is to find a way to guide children toward better behavior while understanding and respecting that each child seeks to use his own will.

It's best in situations involving inappropriate behavior not to be caught off guard but instead to be prepared with a cache of techniques, approaches, and information that will effectively assist you. The goal is for children's behavior to become habitually positive and for you to work yourself out of a job!

Parenting is not for the fainthearted. When your children misbehave it's not okay to throw up your hands and simply hope that the behavior will improve. You need skills, options, and approaches to guide your children down the road to better behavior.

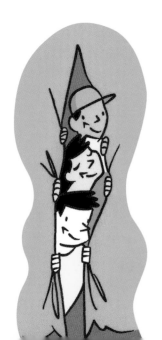

THE ESSENTIAL RULEBOOK FOR MANAGING BEHAVIOR

When your child misbehaves or refuses to comply, refer to this list. You need many approaches at your fingertips. Many of these approaches may already be part of your disciplinary repertoire. Give yourself credit for the ones you use automatically. As you incorporate more and more into your parenting *modus operandi*, you'll feel more competent as you guide your children toward positive social behavior.

Post this list on your refrigerator

1. Describe what your child does that is right. Then move or guide him onto the next activity. To your toddler: "You climbed in your car seat all by yourself today. Good for you. Now please hold my hand in the parking lot." To your sixth grader: "You tidied up the bathroom. You even wiped up the floor after yourself. Thanks so much. Be sure to hang up the damp towel on your bedroom floor."

2. Use proximity control. When your child is beginning to get disruptive, quietly and gently move closer. Often your calm presence raises a child to a higher level of behaving. Whether at a family gathering, when completing homework assignments, or when a friend comes over to play with your child, your proximity often provides positive control without you ever needing to say a word.

3. Redirect your child. If your toddler is touching something he's not supposed to touch, show your child what he can touch. If your child is jumping on the sofa, show him where he can jump. Telling a young child "No, stop it" is not enough. The child may stop for a second, but because his mind isn't particularly flexible, he can't think of something better to do. That's why you need to take it upon yourself to redirect your child to an appropriate activity.

4. Remove an object. If your child is coloring on the wall, remove the crayons. Another time demonstrate how and where to use crayons properly. If your teen's music is too loud, ask him to turn it down. Remove the music player if necessary until he realizes that it's not okay to impose his music choices on the rest of the family.

5. Lay out two realistic expectations. Before going on an airplane or attending Grandma's birthday party, give two realistic expectations about your child's behavior. "When on the airplane, I expect you to keep your seat-belt on and whisper." "Remember, when Grandma opens her presents, you can watch her." With fair warning and clear and reasonable expectations laid out, children usually behave better.

6. Stay away from difficult situations. If going to the grocery store causes problems, go when your spouse or neighbor can watch your child. A month's respite from taking your child to the grocery store is often enough to give you and your child the opportunity to start up a new grocery store routine, and behavior will magically improve. If going to the shopping mall with your teen ends in arguments about what to buy, give it up. It's not worth the misery and it's not good for your relationship.

7. Avoid lots of change all at once. Don't move, fly to Disneyland, and buy a new puppy all in the same month that your child starts child care or high school. Most children—no matter their age—do not have the coping skills to adjust to all that change at once.

8. Remove your out-of-control child. Take him from the scene of the misbehavior. Go for a walk, go to another room, and stay with him until he's calm. Any time your child is disruptive, escorting him away from the situation often gives the anxious child the opportunity to pull himself together and reenter the situation. You're required to remain calm.

9. Provide the control your child lacks. If you want your toddler to get down from the dining room table, say, "I'm not going to allow you to stand on the table. Do you want to get down yourself or do you want me to get you down?" If your tween has exceeded her allotted screen time, state in a clear yet friendly manner, "Your screen time is over for today. Do you want me to turn the computer off or will you do it yourself?" You provide the control. In time, it transfers from you to your child.

10. Give clear commands and demonstrate. Rather than saying, "Put the toys away," it's better to say, "Put the truck in the box. I'll put one in; I bet you can do that, too. I'll watch you." Rather than saying, "Clean your bedroom," it's better to say, "Let's start by putting away all the stuff on the floor and then you can vacuum. Be sure to get under your bed, in the closet, and behind the chair. I'll dust while you vacuum."

11. Look to the next event. "We had fun playing at Jamie's today. In 5 minutes, we're going to get in the car, drive by the fire station, and go to the grocery store." Because children live in the moment, it's tough for them to make the transition from one situation to the next. This fact is particularly true for young children, but even teens like to be apprised of what's happening next on the family's agenda. Knowing that Grandma and Grandpa will be arriving in 15 minutes allows your teen to decide whether to stay or hide in her bedroom.

12. Offer a choice in a "no choice" situation. "You must sit in your car seat. Do you want to look at a book or hold your blanket?" "You will be going to church with us, as always. Do you want to wear your boots or shoes?" When parents give a directive, children are more likely to go along with it if they are given some choice in the matter.

13. Establish rules. Work to establish one or two reasonable rules at a time, and then refer to them.

"We all sit at the dinner table for 20 minutes."

"What's the rule about dinner?"

"Everyone takes their shoes off before coming in the house."

"What's the rule about shoes?"

"No TV and telephone calls between 7 and 8 o'clock each evening. It's homework or reading time."

"What's the after-dinner TV and phone rule?"

Once one new rule is well established, then you can introduce another new one.

14. Give to children in fantasy what they can't have in reality. "You wish you could have a whole plate of cookies. You wish you could eat as many as you like, any time you like. I understand that, but I can't allow it." "You wish you could have a new car just like your friend Jeremy. I know you wish you could drive around in it all over town with your friends. Unfortunately that will not happen. You can drive my car as necessary." This approach is effective because by a describing a child's wishes she feels validated and she actually imagines her wish coming true.

15. Ease transitions. Help your little ones make the transition from one activity or situation to another. Because children have a tough time moving from one activity to another, singing a song to them when getting to the dinner table, to bed, or out the door triggers the event in the child's mind, thereby easing them from one situation to the next.

16. Surrender. When a situation is difficult, when you, your children or the household seem out of control, stop! Sit on a chair or sit on the floor near your children. Breathe deeply and let the tense moment pass. Don't feel you always need a perfect solution to a difficult or unpleasant situation. Sometimes it's better for everyone to simply let the moment pass.

17. Let your child be in charge. Children need the opportunity to be the boss, be in control of a situation, or be in charge of a project. The parent follows the child's lead. It could be building with blocks, planning a slumber party, or working on a science project. Putting a child in charge of certain situations increases the likelihood she will comply with your requests.

18. Engage your child's imagination. Children have wonderful imaginations. Play into that imaginative world for compliance. Say, "Mr. Sock (a puppet) says it's not okay to poke, he likes you to pat the baby." "Your dolly needs a bath; she wants you to take one with her." Such imaginative approaches put your child on the path to good behavior.

KiDs MiSbEhAVinG? folLow tHe ThReE-sTeP aPpRoAcH

Daunted at the prospect of being an effective disciplinarian? Don't be. Your task becomes simpler when you consider taking one of "The three options". Put simply, you have three options for responding when your child is naughty, inappropriate, or out of control:

The three options
1. **Step in and stop** the child from doing what she's not supposed to do.
2. **Step near and guide** the child to better behavior.
3. **Step back and watch** to see if the child can manage the situation herself.

Before reacting to a situation, quickly run through in your mind your three options for discipline. Ask yourself which one is appropriate given the situation at hand. Although you probably won't always get it right, you'll feel more effective when you take time to decide what to do rather than just jumping in without a plan.

Option #1:

Step in and stop the child from doing what's prohibited.

This is the option you choose when there is no choice. In other words, this applies to any situation that involves the child's safety or the family's values.

You won't even have to *think* about taking this option. If a child is running toward a wood-burning stove, you will instantly be out of your armchair to stop the child in her tracks, keeping her safe while saying, "No! Stop! It's hot!" This is a safety issue, and at the moment you have no other option. Parents provide protection until children are old enough to protect themselves.

What if you're dealing with an older child? If a child refuses to do his homework, preferring to play a video game, you could turn off the video game while stating, "Homework comes before video games! I'm turning off the video game until you've finished your assignments." Doing so underlines the family's value that homework takes priority over playing a video game.

Option #2:

Step near and guide the child to manage the situation at hand.

In this situation you might offer the child a choice. Compromise or negotiate with her, attempt to solve the problem together, or teach a skill for better behavior.

If a child grabs a toy from another child's hand, you may choose to step into the scene, take control of the toy, and then demonstrate how to take turns, trade, and borrow objects.

You're teaching skills for sharing and not grabbing. You can later monitor the child in a variety of situations to see if she's gradually catching on to what's expected. Keep in mind that children don't learn from one lesson alone. You will need to repeat lessons in numerous situations before the child consistently exhibits the appropriate or desired behavior. This is the option that takes patience—but the rewards will be satisfying.

Option #3:

Step back and watch to see if the child can manage the situation for herself.

Believe it or not, you don't always need to interfere. Often children can determine how to behave all on their own. Given the opportunity, children often handle situations without reminders or prompting from Mom or Dad. You're not redundant yet, but this is the option that asks you to take a backseat.

Take this situation, for example. A child of five years old, when visiting Grandma's house, may automatically know to take his plate from the table to the counter. If the child doesn't, Mom and Dad can model the correct behavior. Miraculously, the child will most likely do as the parent does. Often parents don't need to say a word and the child will behave as desired. It's called leading by example. Even when you're not thinking about it, you're being a good parent!

Mix and match

Don't feel bound to stick to one of the three options above. If you always step in and stop when a child misbehaves, you prevent your child from learning how to manage situations on her own.

If you always step near and guide, you'll exhaust yourself. There are just too many disciplinary situations to attend to every single one of them. You'll tire yourself, and over-parent your child. Work on one or two better behavior skills at a time. When your child masters one, move on to another.

If you always step back and watch, you're being too permissive. Children need protection and guidance. If left completely to her own devices, a child may flounder and learn an unduly harsh lesson.

By exercising each of "the three options," you will gradually teach your children self-discipline and self-control. Keep in mind that discipline involves guidance, teaching, and training. It's not about punishment or about getting back at the child.

Darn good advice in action: Wesley's parents consider the three-option way

Like most children, Wesley was fascinated with the TV. At two years old, Wesley was on the go without inner controls. His parents wanted him to stay away from the TV "Just because we say so," but Wesley couldn't help himself. His curiosity, drive to copy his parents' behavior, and interest in pushing buttons to see what would happen kept him focused on this fascinating box.

Some days Wesley's parents would stop him in his tracks as he approached the TV. Other days they'd build a barricade around the TV until it was time for Wesley to watch *Barney & Friends*. Some days, they'd throw up their hands in frustration and just let him have the TV. Their use of all these approaches in this one situation involving the TV left Wesley feeling confused by his parents' inconsistency and left his parents feeling ineffective and exasperated.

Finally Wesley's parents decided to consider the three options for discipline.

Option 1: Step in and stop. If Wesley's Mom and Dad chose this option, it would mean that every time Wesley moved toward the TV, one of his parents needed to be up and on the ball to move him away and keep him away from it until he was interested in another activity.

Option 2: Step near and guide. Wesley's parents could choose this option by compromising. They could put the TV out of Wesley's reach. Then when it was time to watch Barney or Elmo, they could lift him up and allow him to push the power button on, and then turn it off when the program was over. With this compromise, Mom and Dad succeed in controlling when Wesley touches the TV, and Wesley is also happy because he gets to learn to use the TV. Ultimately, Wesley's parents are guiding him gradually to use the TV competently and responsibly.

Options 3: Step back and watch. In this case, Wesley's parents could just let him push the buttons on the TV at will. In time, he'd most likely lose interest in the TV set and move on to another activity.

Wesley's Mom and Dad decided on Option 2. With a plan in place, it was easy to carry out this disciplinary situation with consistency. Once again, there was peace on the home front.

So how do I control *my* kid?

No matter the child's age, parents in disciplinary situations can consider which of the three options to use.

● If your preschooler insisted on wearing her bikini swimming suit to nursery school in mid-winter, you'd likely choose Option 2, and compromise. She'd need to wear it with tights and a turtle neck.

● If your school-age child is determined to rearrange her bedroom, you'd probably choose Option 3 and let her to do it while keeping a watchful eye as her plan unfolded.

● If your tween demanded to wear makeup to school, you'd likely resort to Option 2 and compromise by allowing her to wear it on weekends when she's with friends. Make the promise that she can wear makeup to high school.

● If your teen wanted to go on an unchaperoned weekend to the beach with friends, you'd exercise Option 1, "No way! As a responsible parent I can't allow it!"

This three-option approach to discipline takes a little thought, effort, and planning. It's also critical to carry out the plan consistently even if pouts, anger, or temporary unhappiness results.

How to make consequences count

● Make sure the consequence is clearly related to the situation. Let's say William is an hour late coming home from a movie. What's a reasonable consequence? Next week he must come home an hour early. If his parents cancel a fishing trip that's been planned for months, that's not fair.

● Watch your demeanor. There's no need to be harsh and punishing; simply be firm and clear. Your son rides his bike out of your cul-de-sac,

Consequences can bring about positive change

- The action: Little Sean spills his milk.
- The consequence: He cleans it up.

By requiring Sean to wipe up the spill, his parents hope that in the future he'll be more careful. They also hope that Sean gets the message that when he goofs up, he's responsible for remedying the situation. Sean, at age three, is perfectly capable of wiping up spilled milk, so he might as well do it.

What's the consequence if teenager Beth lends a new pair of jeans to a friend who then spills bleach on them? Beth doesn't have the jeans to wear to the dance on Saturday night, as planned. Through this unfortunate experience, Beth learns that clothes loaned out to other people sometimes get ruined. This real-life experience served a purpose, teaching Beth a lesson Mom couldn't.

---

violating your rules. You confidently impose the consequence: "William, you've lost the privilege of riding your bike for three days. After this break from riding your bike, I hope you'll follow the rules again."

- Explain your reason once; don't try to convince your child that what you've done is fair. Just explain the situation, and lock up the bike.
- Realize that any consequence you require your child to bear, you're forced to live with, too. By restricting William from riding his bike, he'll be underfoot for three days instead of outside riding bikes.
- Understand that a brief reprimand from a beloved parent is often consequence enough to produce the desired result.
- When consequences are effective, they're just unpleasant enough to bring about positive change.

PeRfEctiNg thE finE aRt of PrObLeM solvinG

Older brother, age ten, invited a friend to spend the night on Friday. Younger brother, age eight, wants to be included. Older brother's reaction? "No way!"

Here's the procedure for solving this problem:

Describe the Problem. When everyone is in a good mood, sit both boys down at the kitchen table and identify the problem. "On Friday, as you both know, Billy is having Sam spend the night. Billy, you don't want Jeremy around, right? And Jeremy, you want to play and sleep with Billy and his friend, right? And I don't want to put up with any fighting and arguing, so what should we do?"

Brainstorm Ideas. Come up with as many solutions as possible and write them down. All ideas are accepted no matter how outrageous. Let children be imaginative. This encourages their creativity and builds their confidence.

Here are the ideas that the three came up with:

❏ Let Jeremy have a friend over, too.
❏ Send Jeremy to Grandma's for the night.
❏ Let Jeremy have a video to watch while Billy and Sam play.
❏ Let Jeremy be included.
❏ Lock Jeremy in his room.
❏ Cancel plans with Sam.
❏ Let Jeremy be with Billy and Sam on Friday night but not Saturday morning.

Review the Solutions. Decide together which solutions will work and which won't. Everyone must agree.

After much discussion, here's the solution they reached: Jeremy was not allowed to play with Billy and Sam but he could choose a video and watch it with Mom and Dad. Next Friday would be his turn to have a friend over.

After Billy had more time to think, he wanted to revise the agreement. He offered to let Jeremy be included on Friday night if he and his friend could watch the movie, too. But on Saturday morning Billy could have Sam to himself.

Jeremy and Mom agreed to this revision.

Follow Through. It is up to the parent to oversee the evening's events to make sure everything goes as planned. As it turned out, the sleepover was a success without any verbal or physical sibling fights.

You can solve many family disputes with this plan: dividing up chores, planning a family outing, deciding who can sit in the front seat, and solving a fight over a video game.

It's usually best to write down the agreement, because memories often fade and a written record often saves wasted arguments about what everyone really decided.

When children have input—that is, use their brain for problem solving, compromising, and negotiating—they're usually quite willing to carry out the plan with success.

CHApTeR 6
DOn't HaVe
A cRiSis!

EmErGenCy DiScIplInAry TechNiqueS

A rItE oF pAsSaGe— HuMiLiAtIoN iN tHe SuPeRmArKeT

Before having children of your own, you probably witnessed other people's children misbehaving in the supermarket—flying into a tantrum, talking back, and hitting one another. At your last family holiday celebration, your niece possibly bit your nephew when he snatched a toy from her hand. You probably muttered under your breath, "My children will never behave that way."

W ell, now you're walking in those very same parenting shoes as your fellow shoppers or extended family members. You yearn for emergency techniques and approaches to discipline that will help you with these difficult and embarrassing situations. There are approaches to discipline that you can tuck under your parenting belt to pull out when needed, but it's important to be realistic. There will be a time—and probably times— when *your* child will be the one throwing a temper tantrum in a toy store because you won't buy one more plastic truck, or *your* children might be the ones disrupting Grandmother's birthday party. No parent is exempt.

Is humiliation inevitable?

Before diving into a disciplinary situation head first, examine where your children live, learn, and play. Children's bodies are active and their minds are curious. Their brains don't start working when at child-care or school and then stop when home or in public places. They need unstructured downtime involving play and hobbies, but even then, they're still learning. They're eagerly trying to be successful in whatever environment they enter. If they are forced into inappropriate places that don't allow them to use their mind and bodies adequately, they'll resort to misbehavior.

> **Toddlers don't dine, they nibble**
> If you take your toddler to a restaurant and you become furious because your toddler misbehaves, remember, toddlers don't *dine*. Order takeout and dine at home after your toddler is tucked in bed for the night.

If you're shopping with your four- and eight-year-old children, most likely they'll be interested in riding the escalators, running up and down the mall, and playing hide and seek between the clothing racks. It's unlikely they'll behave like little ladies and gentlemen while you pick out a dress for your class reunion.

When you find yourself in an unpleasant situation with your children, just walk away. It's tough to remedy the situation right then. It's best to just give it up for the day and evaluate the circumstances: You may want to wait a few years before trying such an excursion again.

Even in an appropriate environment, you may still see your children exhibit dreadful behavior. The behaviors that parents respond to with horror include biting, grabbing and not sharing, temper tantrums, talking back, hitting, pushing, and kicking. When the child is school-aged, it's lying, stealing, and cheating. And when a tween or teen, the negative behavior ranges from outrageous clothing to an argumentative attitude, to a rebellious attitude toward Mom and Dad's values, ideals, and expectations.

GrAbBiNg AnD nOt ShArInG

Here's a troublesome, yet common scenario: A toddler and a three-year-old are playing together. One grabs a toy from the other, and the other refuses to share. When a parent sees their sweet little child hold onto a toy refusing to give it up to another, Mom or Dad might fear that they're raising a child who's selfish, hoards objects, and who has no sense of generosity or fairness. What could be worse?

While this most likely will be not the case, parents are eager to help their child on the road to sharing and not grabbing.

Typically, when toddlers see an interesting toy, they're curious about how it works, so they grab it. They don't know to say, "May I play with it when you're done?" so they just snatch it away. Your task is tough. On the one hand you want to respect the toddler's immature social skills but you also need to respect the other child's right to not have toys his taken from him.

How to handle a snatch and grab

- Stay no further than two feet away when young children play, intervening quickly when necessary. Do your best to see the play time goes well.
- Don't force a child to share; you'll only make the hoarding and grabbing worse.
- Move near when children start wrangling over a toy. When you're nearby, children often stop arguing and decide on their own how to manage the situation.
- Step in, holding the toy in question, then sit between the children and say, "You both want the shovel, what should we do?"
- Return the toy to the child who had it first. Then tell the child who grabbed that she can have a turn when the child with the toy finishes with it.
- Negotiate a trade: "Carrie would like to play with the blue doll. She'd like to trade it for the pink doll."
- Set a time limit: "In five minutes Carrie can have a turn with the blue doll. I'll set a timer."
- Give the toy a "time out" by putting it high on a shelf for the rest of the playtime.
- Don't expect children to share a special blanket or cuddle toy.

All this refereeing may overwhelm you, but there's no need to lose heart. By age four, most children learn the natural give-and-take of managing objects as they gradually learn to ask for a turn, trade, wait for a turn, and play together cooperatively.

Taming Back Talk

There's no behavior that shocks parents more than a mouthy
child who talks back. You would have never spoken to your
parents that way. What's going on? You probably encouraged your
children to state their opinions and express their feelings, but
because they're kids they don't always know how to express
themselves using respectful language.

Your child says, "I hate going to dinner at Grandma's, you can't
make me go." What she means is, "You know, Dad, there really
isn't anything for me to do at Grandma's. Can I take a video along?" In
both cases, the child is making her point, whether rudely or considerately.

Kids today are definitely not the "seen and not heard" generation.
Unfortunately today children are not only seen and heard but often it's
over and above their parents. Encourage your children to express their
opinions and feelings; just realize it's a long, complicated process for
them to refine their language skills enough to assert their point of view
in a respectful manner. It's important to keep at it. You do your children
a disservice when you allow them to speak uncontrollably. Everyone
benefits when children learn to communicate respectfully.

When your child talks back, when he's rude, sassy, disrespectful, or
mouthy, you need to know how to respond. Here are some options:

❏ **Ask your child to say the very same thing but in a nicer way.**
If a child says, "More milk!" simply say, "Can you ask in a nicer way?"
Given a second chance, kids often improve right away.

❏ **Respond with an acceptable statement.**
When your three-year-old is too blunt and says, "These potatoes are
icky, Grandma. They're making me sick!" just say in an upbeat tone,
"Sam doesn't care for potatoes, but he loves your fruit salad."

❑ **Teach and practice polite language.**

On the way to Grandma's, have your children practice saying, "No, thank you, Grandma. I don't care for mashed potatoes."

❑ **Make sure your family adheres to the family rules.**

When your eight-year-old says, "Doing the dishes is not fair. What am I? Your slave?" Come back with, "That's disrespectful. In our family we don't talk like that."

❑ **Give your child the words to say.**

Your child says crudely, "I'm not wearing that ugly dress; you can't make me." Say, "Please don't talk that way to me. Say this instead: 'I really don't like wearing dresses. Can I wear pants instead?'"

❑ **End the conversation.**

When a child is overly demanding, tell her, "I'm willing to talk with you about anything, but not when you're out of verbal control." End the dialogue with: "The conversation is over for me."

❑ **Avoid shouting back.**

Saying, "Don't you ever talk that way to me," serves no purpose. You don't control the words that come out of your child's mouth.

❑ **Model respectful language.**

If you stand with hands on hips and your finger pointed at your three-year-old while saying, "Get your coat on right now, young lady!" you can be sure your preschooler will use this same communication technique sometime. The rule is simple: Speak to your children in the same manner you expect them to speak to you. It's not only your words but also your body language and tone of voice that matter. Walk over to your child, gently touch her on the shoulder, and say, "It's time to get your coat on. I'm getting mine on, too."

Hitting, kicking, pushing—the three evils

This mom's question reflects the frustration many parents of toddlers and young preschool-aged children experience.

What's a parent to do?

My twenty-one-month-old son, Christopher, pushes, kicks, and hits people when upset. At home I warn him and then isolate him in a playpen for a time out, but what do I do when we're at a playgroup or on the playground?

He acts aggressively for territorial reasons—he wants to be the only one on a slide. Or for possessive reasons—he wants a toy train all to himself. Usually when such situations occur in public, I quickly apologize and then redirect Christopher to another activity. I sometimes feel, however, that it's not really fair that he must leave his fun-filled activity just because another kid comes along.

What's the answer?

Although frustrating, such aggressiveness is typical of many toddlers and three-year-olds. Young children are unskilled in social graces. Some feel threatened when another child innocently approaches their play area or possession.

There's no need to fear that just because your child exhibits these hurtful forms of aggression now, he will always behave this way. He simply doesn't have the social wherewithal to see from another's perspective or play cooperatively. However, you can't just stand there and do nothing.

When you watch toddlers play, notice that about half of the social interactions between them are aggressive. By the time they're age three-and-a-half, there's much less aggression. The main reason is that by then children speak their mind rather than go on the attack.

In fact, some toddlers are innately aggressive, while others are docile. This may be perplexing, but there's no need to ponder at length why some children are more trying on the playground and in play groups than others. Instead, if your child is one of the go-getters, develop a plan to nurture him through this difficult period. In doing so he'll arrive on the other side of age three better able to control himself.

How to handle the three evils:

- Resist meeting her aggression with your aggression. If parents turn aggressive, the child's inappropriate physical attacks will escalate rather than gradually drop out of sight.
- Keep your child from hurting others. When you're at the park or in the playgroup, stay near the aggressive child. Don't give her the opportunity to attack others. You must be in close proximity to step in and stop her from harming others. You can skillfully monitor each situation, ensuring that the aggressive child and the other children are protected.
- Accept the fact that sitting on a park bench and chatting with other parents while your child plays happily cannot be part of your current parenting repertoire.
- Redirect the aggressive child from time to time but also know that you can say, "Christopher has the train right now. When he's finished with it, you can have a turn." Or "Christopher likes being on the slide all by himself. When he slides down and climbs off, then you can climb up."
- Tell the aggressive child who succeeds in hitting, pushing, or kicking that it is not acceptable. Do so whether at home or in public. Use a stern face and voice. Hold his hands and body, preventing him from any more aggressive behavior, and say, "I know you're frustrated but I can't allow pushing."
- Resist isolating the attacker for a time out. Often isolation brings more frustration. Young children need not only physical protection but emotional protection as well. He needs you to prevent or stop his aggressive attacks, but he also needs you near him to validate the emotions that he's experiencing. (See pages 168–75 for appropriate approaches.)

Stop your child in the name of love

Toddlers and many preschool-aged children don't have the self-control to stop themselves from hurting others; that's why they need parents nearby to keep them from hurting others. By the time a child turns three, or possibly a little older, the control you provide naturally transfers from you to him. In time, he'll stop himself and use words, not actions, to express himself in situations that involve territory and favorite possessions.

BiTiNg

What's the worst, most primitive behavior that young children exhibit? It's biting. Although most young children bite once or twice in their careers as toddlers, when it's your child doing the biting, you can't let the incident go without reprimand.

A mom asks about biting

My three-year-old is biting other children at his child-care facility. His biting behavior surfaced at about eighteen months during family holidays and birthday gatherings. His preschool-age cousins were his targets, upsetting everyone. These episodes occurred infrequently and, thankfully, subsided within six months or so. Now at child care, the biting has resurfaced. The child-care provider reports an episode almost daily. How should she and I proceed with discipline so this behavior stops?

What is the answer?

Biting is the toughest aggressive behavior to respond to because it's upsetting for everyone involved—the bitten child, the biting child, the other children watching, and the adult responsible for the children.

Toddlers are easily frustrated and they don't have the language skills to express their frustration, so they sometimes sink their sharp little teeth into the skin of another child. Some toddlers even bite their parents. Biting is not unusual; it's a characteristic particular to toddlers.

Toddlers: what to do

If an incident occurs with only one adult present, put the biter on one side of you and the bitten child on the other. Comfort the bitten child, administer first aid, and allow the biter to watch. The bitten child's care should include an eventual trip to the doctor if the skin has been broken.

Once the bitten child is calm, deal with the biter:

1. Hold the biter, grasp her mouth, and state firmly, scowling your face a bit, "No biting! Biting is dangerous and not allowed."

2. Massage the child's tense mouth to help relax it.

3. Provide an understanding of the situation at hand, "I know you're angry. You didn't like it when Alice took your blanket."

4. Set the limit again: "No biting!"

5. Offer a teething toy, telling the child, "You may bite the toy, but you can't bite people because it hurts them." Toddlers won't understand every word, but they certainly pick up on your facial expression, body language, and tone of voice.

6. Stay with the child until he's calm, and offer a soothing activity such as squishing and pounding play dough or water play. These work magic in calming a distressed child.

Neither the adult managing the situation nor the bitten child should bite back. It's not right to teach children proper behavior by demonstrating improper behavior. Biting is wrong for everyone at all times.

You want to proceed in such a way that biting will soon drop out of sight. Punishment and harsh violent measures only contribute to the child's frustration and may cause the child to bite more.

No matter what his age, if your child occasionally bites, it's best to shadow him when he's near other children. That way you'll be right there to step in and prevent another biting incident from occurring.

**Biting: An ounce of prevention is better than a
pound of cure**

Watch for what happens right before biting occurs. Try to
find out what provoked the bite. By doing so, you might be able
to change the environment to prevent biting from occurring.

Watch for crowding. When young children play in close
proximity and in a small play space without adult supervision, the
likelihood is greater that a biting incident will occur.

Watch for over-stimulation. If children are becoming over-
stimulated, a biting incident might take place. Take the over-
stimulated children to play with water, play dough, or sand.

Notice if children are hungry or tired. A child is more likely
to bite because he is hungry or tired. To avoid this, give him a
nutritious snack and allow him to rest on his bed or on your lap.

Preschoolers: what to do

For children older than three, use a different tactic. For preschool-aged
children who can talk when frustrated but who continue to bite, your
approach should be a tad more severe than when a toddler bites.
Biting has become a habit because, for some reason, it is a successful
tactic for the child. When a child bites in a group setting, the adult
needs to attend to the bitten child but almost simultaneously isolate
the biter in a quiet spot for three minutes.

When the child bites, say, "I know you're frustrated, but biting is
not allowed." When her three-minute time out is over, bring her back
into the group of children, offer lots of attention for positive actions

while keeping an eye on her, providing an air of protection. Move her from any potentially explosive circumstances that may lead to biting.

Every time the child bites, the care provider should proceed in exactly the same manner. The child is not to receive anything from biting except exclusion from the group for three minutes—that means no attention. Children want to be part of the group and receive attention; the parent or care giver's job is to help them do so in a way that is positive and pleasant, rather than hurtful.

If you follow this procedure, biting behavior should stop.

Watch out—A Temper Tantrum's On Its Way!

You've either experienced it or witnessed it…a mom and tot at the grocery store. Mom is trying to do her shopping. Toddler is trying to touch, open, smell, and taste everything, and take it home. When she's told to stop this, the classic temper tantrum takes place—wails, screams, tears, and flailing arms and legs.

It's so embarrassing. Everybody's staring at you, criticizing and judging. "Why can't that mom control her child?"

You would like to cry and flee. But you know you can't do that. Thankfully, there are other options. But realize, once a temper tantrum has taken off in a public place, there are few perfect solutions.

You can go to the car and let the child calm down and try shopping again in a few minutes. Or you can go home and shop when you can be by yourself. Or you can zoom around the aisles with the wailing child and get your shopping done as quickly as possible, ignoring all the glares and raised eyebrows.

Can such scenes be avoided? Is this normal?

Some tantrums can be avoided, and, yes, for children between eighteen months and three years tantrums are normal. Toddlers have between three and five tantrums a day, while preschool-aged children have about one per week. Young children simply have a low tolerance for frustration. When they want to complete a puzzle but can't, they scream. When they're having fun playing and it's suddenly time for bed, they stomp.

Toddlers aren't able to say, "I'm angry, this puzzle is too hard." They don't have the skill to say, "Just give me five more minutes, then I'll go to bed without a problem." So they show their frustration with rage.

When children are tired or hungry, tantrums come more easily. Shopping malls, restaurants, and grocery stores are inappropriate environments for most young children. Here children are expected to behave beyond their age and ability. When this happens, tantrums occur with frequency.

To reduce the chance of your child having a temper tantrum, give her lead time from one activity to the next. "In five minutes we'll be going home." "When the timer goes off in ten minutes, it's time for you to go to bed."

If you take your child to a restaurant, make sure she is rested and fed. Also, bring along a simple activity, and plan to attend to your child rather than your meal.

Shopping can be successful if you have lots of time to include your child in the outing. Talk about what you're seeing and doing, and let your child "help."

However, sometimes tantrums just can't be avoided. Here's a typical scene. Your child wants a cracker. You sit her at the table, get the cracker, and it breaks as you set it on the table. The child expected a whole cracker not a broken one—a tantrum erupts. Once begun, it will probably have to run its course. Don't desert or isolate the tantruming child; you need to stay near to provide emotional protection. Yet you don't want to offer undue attention, either. It's a fine line you walk.

Avoid trying to talk your child out of his tantrum. He can't hear reason, logic, or explanations when throwing a tantrum. Try to resist throwing one yourself, although sometimes you'll feel like it.

Some children need to be held during their tantrum. This helps them get over it, because being so out of control is scary. This approach is tough, but you must try to hold the flailing child while keeping yourself emotionally detached.

Some children at the height of the tantrum refuse comfort, but as the wails reduce to whimpers that's your signal to move in with hugs, holding, and rocking.

All children need parents to reflect their feelings. "You don't like broken crackers. Broken crackers make you angry." Since you're using words, in time your child will, too.

How to guarantee a tantrum

There are three factors that keep tantrums occurring beyond the normal age range:

1. If parents give in to a child's demands. If you buy that bag of cookies at the grocery store that your child wants to stop that the tantrum, your child will learn very quickly that tantrums are the key to getting what she wants.

2. If parents throw tantrums when angry and frustrated, children will, too. If you express these feelings in a civilized way with words, your children will eventually learn by your example.

3. If tantrums are given lots of attention, they will become an uncontrollable monster. Children need attention; give it to them when they exhibit positive, pleasant behavior.

A young child's life is filled with frustration. There's no way to eliminate feelings of frustration, nor would you want to. Children will not learn to function in this world if parents are constantly trying to make it frustration-free. But once your child can express this frustration with words rather than tantrums, you'll breath a deep sigh of relief.

Too mAnY tImE oUtS

Today's disciplinary panacea is a technique known as "time out." Many parents feel frustrated with time outs as they seldom result in better behavior.

Okay. So what is time out?

Here's how it typically works. A young child misbehaves by hitting, grabbing, screaming, throwing objects, or talking back. The parent then sets the child in a designated spot for a period of time. This could be on the stairs in the hallway, on a chair facing the corner of the kitchen, or in the child's bedroom.

And time out is meant to work because . . . ?

The theory behind the discipline is that the child will not like sitting on the chair or being alone, so this will stop the hitting, grabbing, screaming, throwing objects, or talking back.

If such time outs result in improved behavior, all is well and good; using the time out method for discipline was effective. If, however, such periods of isolation evoke unnecessary frustration and deteriorating behavior from the child, then it's best to rethink the conventional use of time out.

Rather than isolating a child when he misbehaves, scold him briefly by saying, "Hitting is not allowed." Take him to a quiet spot and stay with him. Once he is calm, offer suggestions for how he can improve his behavior.

By remaining with the child, you're telling him that his behavior was not acceptable but you still love him. If a parent puts his child repeatedly in a time out spot without any suggestions for how he can improve his behavior, the child is left alone feeling terrible about what he did but without the knowledge of how to change his actions for the better.

An alternative use of time out is simply to move the child away from the person, place, or thing that is contributing to the misbehavior.

Time out from a person

If siblings are fighting over who gets to drink from the blue-flowered cup, give them a time out from one another by separating them until they calm down, and then offer suggestions for resolving the dispute.

Time out from a place

If a child is misbehaving at a family holiday celebration, give him a time out from the situation by sitting with him in a bedroom until he composes herself. Once the child has collected himself, offer a couple of expectations for improved behavior and allow him to reenter the gathering.

> **Time out from an object**
> If a child uses a toy hammer on the coffee table, take it away. Give the child a time out from using the hammer and then later show him where and how he can use it.

Another approach to time out is to notice when a child is on the verge of misbehaving. Sometimes a parent can see a child welling up with frustration—ready to explode or do something mischievous. At that point the parent can say, "Let's go to your bedroom and read a story." This might be all it takes for the child to pull his emotional and behavioral self back together.

After reading the story, the parent might say, "Now stay in your room for a little while, look at some books, and then come out into the kitchen when you're feeling better." If the child is willing to stay in his cozy bedroom surrounded by stuffed animals and books for a quiet time out, he learns to manage feelings of angst without causing disruption and further negative repercussions to himself and others.

Take care when employing time out. If a child exhibits feelings of self-loathing, stop using time out. Shunning or shutting a child off can prompt lack of confidence. Time out backfires when a child says things like: "I hate myself." "No one likes me." "I wish I were never born." There are many approaches to time out; each is effective only when the child's behavior improves and the child continues to exhibit good mental health.

Other forms of time out

Toy time out: When a child misuses a toy, give the toy a time out.

Friend or sibling time out: When children are not getting along, they need to take a time out from one another.

Holding time out: Hold the child to end the misbehavior or to help her regain control. Then assist her in re-entering the group or situation.

Talking time out: Take the child away from the scene of the misbehavior, and when the child is calm, talk about alternatives for better behavior.

Walking time out: Take a disruptive or angry child outside to walk or run around for a few minutes. Any form of exercise— swinging or riding a rocking horse—can help the out-of-control child gain composure.

Group time out: If the day is not going well, change the tone by going on a walk, getting out some play dough or playing with water, or putting on some lively music and dancing.

Adult time out: The parent takes a time out because she's overwhelmed. Take a parenting break for a few minutes or, if possible, a few hours.

Resting time out: If the parent senses a child is beginning to get antsy and out of control, escort him to a quiet spot, read him a story, and then have him look at a few books alone to calm down.

Build your child's conscience

Let's say your ten-year-old is tempted to steal a pack of gum from a convenience store, but doesn't. What stops him? Is it the fear of being caught and getting into trouble with the store owner, the police, and you? Or does he stop because he knows it's wrong to take something that doesn't belong to him?

Regardless of the reason, it's his conscience that keeps him from slipping the gum into his pocket. The conscience tells children to do what's right, even when no one is watching. Developing a conscience doesn't just happen. Kids do not acquire control over their impulses without teaching, interference, and limits from parents and other significant adults.

Many parents quite naturally go about building their children's conscience. If you're not sure you're doing an effective job and don't want to leave the process to chance, there are two emotions which can help you guide your child.

Pride

Let your children know what brings you pride. When any of your kids do something that in your eyes is right, let him see the adoration and approval on your face. Then underline your pride with words.

When your preschooler, without a reminder, carries his plate from the table to the counter after dinner, say, "I see you're taking your plate from the table to the counter. What a helper. Thank you." When you exhibit pride in such situations, your child learns that helping and responsibility are right.

When your eight-year-old daughter runs home with the news she broke the neighbor's window while playing baseball, inform her that she will need to use her allowance to pay for it. Then be sure to

display pride by saying, "The most important part of this incident is that you came to me with the truth. I'm so proud of you."

As children get older, and they no longer need to hear your approval, they feel pride in doing what's right all on their own. The power of parental pride transfers from parent to child. They do what's right automatically; it's the positive voice of their conscience talking.

Guilt

When your child does something you believe is wrong, reprimand him. Inflict a little guilt. Guilt imposes an uneasy feeling that relates to parental disapproval. Don't, however, paralyze your child with guilt. Use it in small and appropriate doses, building a healthy conscience.

Let's say your children are playing Monopoly and one child is cheating. Say:

"I saw you cheat. You took $500.00 from the bank. That's not okay. Put it back. I'm really sorry to see you take advantage of your little brother."

That's all you need to do. Many such incidents and messages add up to building a child's conscience and self-control.

Parents have the power to use pride and guilt to teach children right from wrong. Use your power wisely and responsibly. Keep your expectations realistic. Realize you'll need to teach lessons of right and wrong over and over again.

One mom's solution

Here's what one mother did when her six-year-old son picked a bunch of tulips from their neighbor's garden. She reprimanded him by saying, "No, I don't approve of you picking flowers from other people's flower beds. Mr. Smith planted those. They're his to pick, not yours." She went on like this for 30 to 45 seconds, and then stopped.

The child felt bad about what he did. Then Mom let up by saying, "We're going to Mr. Smith's to apologize. Then we'll take some of your allowance and buy some flowers to replace the ones you picked."

At first, the child experienced guilt. By apologizing and making up for what he did, his guilt is relieved. This experience and others teach him it's not OK to take what is not his.

An important point to remember is that excessive guilt can lead to shame. If the mother had gone on and on about the tulips, making her son feel that what he did was catastrophic and unforgivable, he would have imposed shame. Bringing up the incident again and again would have reinforced this shame. Shame serves no purpose and simply makes a child feel she's bad. It's much better to reprimand him and let him know what he did was wrong, then provide an avenue for him to make up for it.

Tweens and teens

There's much to learn about adolescents' behavior and their need to establish themselves as separate from their mom and dad. You'll save your sanity and keep your tween or teen safe when you:

• Communicate information they need to hear in sound bites. Resist the urge to lecture. Try saying:

"Passionate displays of affection in public are not OK."

"That blouse is too revealing. You can't wear it to school."

"If your friends drink alcohol in your car, you're responsible. It's against the law."

• Expect some rebellion. If it's safe rebellion (messy bedroom, unique language) let it pass; if it's dangerous (drugs, skipping school, sneaking out), get help from a professional.

• Debate with your adolescent about the values that they're questioning. Such discussions—politics, the environment, religion—are a way of bonding with your teen. Besides, your tweens and teens need to hear, and deep down really want to know, your point of view. They just can't tell you that.

• Take care of yourself by saying inside your own head, "I'm fine. My child will be fine. This difficult time will pass."

CHApTeR 7

EArLy
LeArNinG

The "what happens if I push this?" factor

Young children don't learn by merely observing life around them; they use all their senses and motor ability to learn about the world. When they see a ball, they want to feel it, taste it, listen to the noise it makes, determine how it moves, and smell the material it's made of. Then they want to watch the ball knock things over and ricochet off floors and walls. When they are about eighteen months old, they check to see your reaction to the ball bouncing off windows, floors, walls, and stairwells. Are you going to respond with horror, interest, exasperation, or glee?

Toddlers are on the go with no inner controls, and they like to make things happen. They pull strings to make lights go on and off, push buttons to turn the TV on and off, and turn dials to hear music louder and then softer. There will be many days when you wish your toddler had come with a pause button of his own and you could push it for just five minutes.

Toddlers are so busy exploring the world around them; no parent can take an eye off them for even a second. Eighteen-month-old children are little scientists and psychologists testing their hypotheses about such substances as water, milk, and juice and then watching the parent's reaction as they deliberately spill that substance on the floor.

Locks and keys

A child nearly two years old was fascinated with locks and keys. What toddler isn't? They *are* fascinating; keys open up doors and start cars. Dead bolt locks secure a door that even a key can't open.

One rainy day when the toddler's mom was still in her bathrobe, she stepped outside to empty the garbage. The toddler quickly decided to test a hypothesis: "When the doors are dead bolted from the inside, someone outside can't enter the house." He found his theory to be true, and his mom could not re-enter the house.

There Mom stood, wondering what in the world to do, but she knew it wouldn't help to panic. She pantomimed from outside the window to undead bolt the lock. Once the child had verified his hypothesis, he toddled to the door and unlocked it, allowing Mom to come in out of the rain. She breathed a sigh of relief.

Such incidents occur minute-by-minute with toddlers. You might think that their actions are random and haphazard. They're not. Toddlers observe, think, reason, balance evidence, and draw conclusions about everything they encounter. They learn by doing. It's called play, and it's critical to children's learning. Don't worry about the need to stimulate your child's mind; instead, notice what your child is drawn toward—it could be playing with a jack-in-the-box or stacking cups or opening and shutting cupboards and drawers again and again. Make sure the child is safe, and allow him to master each object's use and purpose.

PlAyInG iS a VeRy SeRiOuS bUsInEsS

If you're a parent who takes your toddler or preschool-aged child to an after-school class—be it ballet, music, gymnastics, or an academic preschool—and you do so because you believe this schedule will provide the best brain-enriching experiences, you might want to reconsider. Instead, or in addition, do what you can to support your child's imaginative play by offering space, uninterrupted time, and props to enhance that play.

After taking your child to the fire station, realize that he'll best absorb and make sense of the experience if he can reenact it in imaginary play. Preschoolers who spend more time in dramatic play are more advanced not only in general intellectual development but also in their ability to concentrate for long periods of time.

Some parents seem skeptical that play, which looks to some like merely a pleasant pastime, can really be the most intellectually stimulating activity that children do. Parents need to understand that there's a big difference between how they and young children learn. For instance, if you're curious about what a doctor does in his work, you ask questions and read to gain an understanding of his occupation. Your preschooler doesn't learn as you do; after a visit to the doctor he needs to reenact the experience. You help out by providing a doctor's kit and then just watch as your child relives through play the visit to the doctor's office. And don't be surprised if you're recruited to be the patient!

When siblings recreate a trip to Mom's office, they work together remembering what they experienced, thus building their memory. They'll pretend to use a copy machine, scanner, and laptop computer.

Other benefits of imaginative play

Pretend play not only enhances intellectual development but also exercises all facets of the developing child. Here's how:

Social Ability

Children's social skills—sharing, taking turns, conversing—increase as they work out the intricacies of a play theme with friends or siblings. Also, children rise to a higher level of social ability when playing. Set up a tea party, and notice how considerate and polite each child becomes in this play scene.

It's amazing to observe. A child who seems to flit from one activity to another will, when playing imaginatively, play longer with more complex themes, be thoroughly involved, and even be more cooperative than in other situations.

Emotional strength

New feelings confuse children. By pretending to be disappointed, fearful, angry, or jealous in play, children come to manage and understand those feelings. In addition, after engaging in pretend play involving emotions, children miraculously learn to empathize with others who show those emotions.

Creativity

In the world of pretend play, children can be anyone and do anything. Predictably, children who spend lots of time engaged in such play score high on tests of imagination and creativity.

Discipline

Imaginative play even helps with discipline. When your child tells her teddy bear, "No, you can't eat another cookie, you'll spoil your appetite," understand that by stepping into the role of disciplinarian she becomes more disciplined herself.

You can use imaginative play to your advantage, too. Having trouble getting your three-year-old to stop whining? Take a paper cup, turn it upside down, draw a face, and put a "W" on its tummy with a slash going through it. This is the "no whining" puppet. Once the whining starts, bring out the puppet and use a deep voice to tell how he doesn't like whining as it hurts his ears. Watch your child collect herself and interact with the puppet.

Difficult situations

Are you moving into a new house? Will a new baby arrive at your home soon? Are you going back to work and is your child starting child care? Are you starting to teach your child to use the toilet? If so, locate a couple of dolls and use them to create scenarios that lay out the change that will occur in your child's life. Difficult childhood situations can add stress to a preschooler's life. Pretend play offers a release that can help children overcome their fears and any misunderstandings they may have.

After the birth of her brother, five-year-old Anna pretended to give birth to five dolls in the dining room of her home. After each birth she'd make a bed for the baby, nurse it, diaper it, and then start the process all over again.

Make pretend play even better

1. Find the royal you! Play the role of prince when your daughter steps into the role of princess. Let her be in charge. Don't take over by questioning, instructing, or intruding. Simply watch, listen, and play along. You'll learn lots about your child.

2. Allow your children to transform your dining room table into a fort. Let it stay up a few days so the fort theme can develop and extend over a period of time.

3. Go out of your way to bring in same-aged playmates. As your child moves into the third year, a playmate satisfies and supports her world of make believe. It's not until a child is seven that she can play well with more than one child at a time.

4. Try not to interrupt children's play. If you must take your astronaut to the grocery store, let her stay in her space suit for the excursion. When it's time to eat lunch, maybe she can eat in her closet-turned-space-capsule.

5. When you search for a preschool for your child, notice if the curriculum provides for and values pretend play. Is there a housekeeping corner, a grocery store, a block corner?

6. Play along if your child creates an imaginative playmate. Often children use imaginative friends as an emotional counterpart: The shy child may create a friend named Gagas who is brave and outgoing. Go ahead and set a place for Gagas at the table, but if he's blamed for throwing food on the floor, say, "Gagas is pretend. He didn't throw food on the floor, you did."

The theater of your child's imagination

Offer an array of objects and props that support your child's world of make-believe. Put together prop boxes for your kids with three or four props that help get your child's play theme under way. Then, as the child's interest dwindles, add another theme-related item to restimulate the play. After a trip to the fire station, provide a toy fire truck, a helmet, and a piece of hose. Later add a walkie-talkie and a toy ambulance. Go to the library together and find a book about fire fighters.

Grocery store
- Paper bags
- Toy cash register
- Play money
- Empty cereal boxes, clean plastic cartons and yogurt pots

Doctor's office
- Medical kit
- Bandages
- Dolls
- Tongue depressor
- Ace bandage

Note: When interest in the doctor's office subsides, pull out stuffed animals and make it a veterinary office.

Business office
- Keyboard
- Telephone
- Tablet of paper
- Envelopes
- Adhesive notes
- Hole puncher

Materials to support all play themes
- Blankets
- Big, empty boxes
- Wood scraps
- Masking tape
- String
- Cardboard
- Large paper
- Discarded paper towel rolls

Artist Studio
- Plastic scissors
- Paper
- Marking pens
- Glitter
- Glue
- Discarded wrapping paper and ribbon
- Tape
- String
- Paint

Note: Keep a watchful eye for items to add to the studio. Keep it tidy but rich with interesting items to include in art projects.

Writing Supplies
- Fat pencils
- Lined paper
- Stapler for assembling books
- Crayons
- Stickers
- Stamps with pads

Note: Often a child will draw a picture and then he'll need you to take down his dictation to caption the picture he drew.

Tune into kid's play and learn something

Five-year-old Erica and six-year-old Alan spend most summer afternoons playing together. On Monday they created a hotel and recreation complex out of blocks. It took them three hours to develop this architectural wonder.

That week they had heard of an earthquake in California, so in the tradition of Frank Lloyd Wright, there was lots of discussion and preparedness for earthquakes. They conducted many trial shakes to test how well their structure would withstand a quake measuring 8.2 on the Richter scale.

Also included in their complex was an elaborate use of signs. These were works of art as well as useful items.

And then the people and cars arrived. Lego families poured into the England and Faull Hotel in everything from dune buggies to space ships. Some visitors arrived by helicopter which could zoom into an upper floor lobby landing spot, while others arrived by boat.

Where did all this play take place? In the living room. Yes, by anyone else's standards, it's a mess. But to these developers it represents hours of work. A week later it was still standing.

Where was Mommy?

The mom in charge was free each afternoon during construction. The kids were so involved that they needed only a parent to assist with spelling for the signs and to show interest in their creation. She busied herself with gardening, reading, and her own hobbies.

But what were the kids learning?

First of all, when kids build with blocks they are laying the foundation for math. They learn that two smaller blocks put together make one larger block. Two halves make a whole, or one plus one makes two; and then it gets more complicated. Their math knowledge was not gleaned from a textbook; it was hands on, concrete, the way young children learn best.

Block play not only lays the foundation for math, but physics and architecture are involved, too. And there was so much planning—this was no haphazard fly-by-night complex. These builders prepared their hotel for the space age.

With the signs, they were practicing their reading and writing skills, and the entire project pushed their creative ability to the limit.

The art of negotiation

Then there were the conversations between these two builders. Both had definite ideas about their project. They did some negotiating but neither wanted to compromise their ideas. So they divided up the blocks (math, again) and each was assigned a section of the structure to complete.

When it came to making the complex function together, they did need to compromise. Each worked independently, yet each served as a consultant to the coworker's project. These two were practicing for the "real-life" work assignments that will come later in their lives.

The afternoon of play was not frivolous; it was productive and the TV was off. The value of this afternoon could be matched only by the entrepreneurial endeavor that took place the next day . . .

The lemonade stand
Plans for this project had been taking place for days. There was big talk about how they would set up, market, and divide up the labor and capital.

Erica provided the lemonade; and Alan, the cups. They made signs and decorated their coolers, which served a dual role of keeping ice frozen and providing the stand.

Their marketing strategies were amazing. They went door-to-door passing out notices with prices and times of operation. They called on their creative ability once again when they made signs and placed them strategically around the neighborhood. They even make a recording with a little jingle to attract sales.

When they took their business door-to-door, they were both surprised at the tips they received from their generous neighbors. Here they learned something about personal service.

They make $4.75 that afternoon, divided up their profits, and prepared for the next day's operation. But the next day was hot, there was no traffic, and no people were walking by: No business. After about an hour, they went out of business—another learning experience.

Children need your help to set up their play projects and to get ideas, but then you should back off and let them proceed. Stay close by and check to see how things are going; but you should mostly just act as an interested observer.

Word-By-Word, Children Travel The Road to Literacy

What parent doesn't expect that their children will learn to read? To accomplish this task, some parents force-feed their young children, encouraging them to recognize letters and their accompanying sounds. Although recognizing letters and their sounds is key to reading, this is only part of the process.

The road to literacy begins when parents first talk to their babies. Even though the baby doesn't understand the words, she still engages in conversations that involve a give and take of babbling and cooing. This, in time, leads to word sounds. The first is usually some form of "ma ma" and "da da." When parents hear these words, there's a flutter of excitement that reinforces these first verbal milestones.

As parents read to their babies, the tots recognize familiar objects. It's intriguing and gratifying to a baby to see pictures of balls, people, and dogs, symbols of objects they see every day.

The magical world of picture books

Reading storybooks is the next step to literacy. Hearing a story such as *Goodnight Moon* by Margaret Wise Brown read night after night is satisfying to even the youngest toddler.

Then there's a time in preschool or early elementary school when children request that Mom or Dad take down their dictation to capture a thought on paper, inspired by, for example, their own artwork or a trip to the zoo.

Another literacy step is when children memorize entire picture books by their own volition. Even though this step is not really reading, it's significant. The child sees the written word, follows the words with her finger, and recites phrases from memory. She has made an important connection between the words, language, and story line.

Then, without much teaching or tutoring, children begin to recognize letters, make their accompanying sounds, and decode common words, for example, their own name, a store sign, or "c-a-t."

Although these steps excite most parents, there's much more to the big literacy picture.

Creating a reading-rich environment

Parents can do this by reading on their own and to their children, discussing what they're reading, and taking children to the library. Locate books—fiction and nonfiction—on topics that interest children, such as trains, lizards, or planets.

Surround your children with love, interest, and excitement when reading to them. Then when they learn to read for themselves, they'll carry these pleasant feelings with them.

Read to your children

Do so at night before going to sleep and in the morning before going off to play or heading out the door to work, school, or child care. Even when children can read for themselves, parents and children can read a book together—either aloud or silently. Then talk about the characters, storyline, settings, and even the moral of the story. With teens, parents can read aloud stories from the newspaper. For insights into your teen's academic life, ask what they're reading in school.

There's no better way to secure your child's success in school than to read to and with them. And because reading is about comprehension, talk about the content of what you are both reading.

Turn the TV off

TV, videos, and the Internet compete with reading time as well as play and downtime. It's best if you start when your children are young to establish that Mom and Dad control TV, videos, and the Internet. These are powerful influences in the lives of children. They can easily dominate a child's life; some children even become addicted to watching TV and videos, and interacting with the Internet and playing video games. Should you ban them completely? Some parents do. Others establish rules to live by.

Here are some for you to consider establishing in your home:

- No TV, Internet, or videos on weeknights.
- No screen time after school until after dinner.
- No TV, videos, or Internet between 7 and 8 P.M.; this time is designated for homework.
- Parents and children watch TV together and explain what you're viewing.
- No Internet access or TV and videos in children's bedrooms.

There's lots children can learn from watching TV but there's also lots that can confuse them. Even if you control programs that involve sex and violence, there are topics like promiscuous sex, war, rape, murder, and terrorism that can rob children of their childhoods. Are you prepared to explain these topics to your children? Will they understand? If not, make sure they're not exposed to them on TV or through the Internet. Policing TV and Internet exposure is a fulltime parenting job today.

Keep books open around and about your home

While it's important to include reading as part of the bedtime routine, don't compartmentalize reading to this time alone. Whatever you do—cook, garden, or travel—open a book for help and insight. In time, your children will do the same.

It won't be too long until you witness your children learning about people, places, and events from books. You'll know you have a reader when a child chooses to read for entertainment and knowledge. What's important is not *when* children learn to read but rather that they choose to do so.

Naturally, you want your children to be successful in school and to satisfy their curiosity, so there's nothing more important than to nurture the love of reading by making it an overriding value in the home.

ChOOSiNg A pReScHOOl Or ChIlD-cArE cEnTeR

When you seek out a child-care center or a preschool for your child, make sure you're keeping in mind the best interest of your child. If you live with the notion that your child's acceptance to Harvard will be guaranteed by an early learning academic program, it's time to reexamine your approach to preschool and child care.

There is lots of interest today in sending children to early learning programs. Some preschools take up 6 hours in a child's week, others 20; some involve 8-hour programs daily with more intense academics in the morning and a more relaxed program in the afternoon. Do these schools give children the academic edge now and into the future? It's tough to say for sure. What children do need for sure are appropriate environments that stimulate their minds and support the child's intellect and curiosity. This environment can be at home, in school, or a reasonable combination of the two. Learning at home and learning at school needs to be right for the child's age, temperament, and interests.

Hands down, the more parents are interested in their child's education, whether at home or at school, the better the child learns. So, support your child's learning at home and be involved in their school. When you do so the likelihood is great that they will reach their intellectual and academic potential. You can't make your child smarter than his genetic makeup but there's much teachers and parents can do together to help each child develop and use her mind optimally.

So how do you go about finding the right early learning program for your child? Start by watching your child, knowing her personality, and then choosing a preschool that suits it. If your child is overly stimulated by kids, noise, and lots of activity, a child-care center or preschool may not be right for her. She may do better in a child-care home or in a home preschool with some structure but fewer children and less stimulation.

What's right for you?

First note that there are a wide variety of preschools appealing to different program philosophies, interests, and budgets. Know your child and know yourself. What appeals to you and what will appeal to your child? The truth is, if you like the preschool or child-care center, you'll be more inclined to support it with your time, interest, and approval, and that is what makes the difference for a quality preschool experience for your child.

Parents want their children to be enthusiastic about school. Essentially, if you're enthused about your child's school, and get involved, the likelihood will be great that your interest and eagerness will pass from you to your child.

When choosing a school, it's critical that the the one you pick will support the child's natural curiosity. Preschool-aged children seek out what they need to know about the world around them of their own accord. Early learning centers should provide learning experiences to satisfy, not take away from, innate inquisitiveness.

Taking tours

Most areas have a wide variety of preschools. You must do your homework to find the one that's right for you and your child. Start by talking to friends and family members. Make a list, call around, and then go and observe a few programs. When you observe potential preschools or child-care centers, here are some things to look out for:

❑ **Hands-on experiences providing cause-and-effect learning.** Youngsters need to manipulate toys with buttons and levers to understand how to make them work; their minds thrive when they can plant seeds in the ground to see how rooting occurs; they're intellectually stimulated when they build with blocks over and over and eventually understand that a strong foundation supports a taller building.

❑ **Opportunities to play imaginatively.** To incorporate an experience into his mind, a preschool-aged child needs to reenact it through play. After a visit to a bakery, the children will benefit if the early learning environment contains props to extend the experience through imaginative play.

❑ **Expectations for self-help.** The three to five-year-old child is fully prepared to manage the rudiments of daily living. In the school setting, children need to be encouraged to take off and hang up coats, take out and put away toys, set out and clean up snacks.

❑ **Creative experiences with a variety of materials.** During the early years children learn the properties of water, dough, paint, goop, and sand. They enjoy the process of learning to cut, paste, and sprinkle. The materials, not the teacher, will dictate what the child does.

❑ **Time to play with other children.** In the housekeeping corner and the building-block area, children learn to get along in a group as they play cooperatively. Sometimes anger, aggression, or disappointment occurs. In the process, social skills build up along with problem-solving and compromising.

❑ **Places to run, climb, ride, and jump.** Children's bodies require exercise to develop their large motor skills. Indoor and outdoor opportunities for moving around provide a critical part of the preschool curriculum.

❑ **Safe, clean, uncrowded, and a reasonably uncluttered environment.** Safety is essential. Whereas perfect order inhibits children's creativity, a chaotic environment tries young children's sensibilities. Too many toys, too much noise, too many kids together in too small a space equates to confusion, rowdy play, and possibly aggression.

Most important: the caregiver

When it comes down to it, the caregivers/teachers are the most important part of the early learning environment. When you go to visit a preschool or child-care center, notice if the caregivers/teachers are attentive and responsive as well as warm and caring. You want them to treat each child with respect. Look for a person who attends quickly to a child's needs and questions. A quality child-care provider keeps her eyes on the children, knowing when to step in and attend to the children and when to let them play without interference.

Caregivers/teachers need to talk with the children, read to them, and listen to what they have to say. They need to provide interesting things for the children to do, noticing their interests while guiding them as they satisfy their curiosity and explore their world. Good caregivers/teachers are skilled at guiding children's behavior in positive ways.

Then you need to ask yourself: How will my child respond to these caregivers? Are these people and is this place fit for my child's interests and personality?

Can you feel a happy vibe?

Another element to notice is the emotional climate of the child-care center or preschool. Your child is emotionally connected to you, but in order for your child to thrive in the early learning program, that emotional link between child-care provider and child must be there as well. If the environment is emotionally cold, your child will feel lonely, not bonded or attached to the people who are looking after her.

No one can be your clone, but a good parental substitute needs to respond to your child's developing abilities and interests, and that means connecting on an emotional level with each child. When your child is joyful, sad, afraid, distressed, disgusted, surprised, or interested in someone or something, will a caregiver be there to tune in and respond by sharing that emotion with your child? Will she use her face, words, tone of voice, and body language to do so?

Before leaving your child anywhere, observe, ask questions, and provide information about your child. You also need to check the preschool's or child-care's references. This means talking to parents whose children are currently enrolled or whose children have attended in the past. Additionally, check to see if they're licensed. Every state has different licensing requirements for child-care centers and preschools. You can ask about accreditation as well. The accreditation to seek is from the National Association for the Education of Young Children. Once you've chosen a place, support your caregiver/teacher with your time and interest. The partnership between you and your child's caregiver/teacher is critical to your child's well-being.

HoW tO cReAtE yOuR vErY oWn LiFeLoNg LeArNeR

Behind every child setting out on her first day of school is a parent who hopes that she'll succeed academically. What does academic success mean to you and to your child?

To put your child's academic life in perspective, look at it from three angles.

Learn to dig learning

What is academic discipline? It occurs when children acquire good study habits related to school work: Completing assignments in class, listening to and following teachers' instructions, and taking responsibility for finishing homework.

Through academic discipline, children acquire the heart and soul of their academic life: Spelling, penmanship, grammar, computation, reading comprehension, historical facts, scientific data, and geography. From these mechanics and facts, children gradually develop concepts and an understanding of the world around them.

Have you even seen your child "dig in" or "wrap himself around a topic?" It occurs when your child makes a subject his own. Your child's teacher might have taught him the multiplication tables, but he gets especially turned on, fascinated, and intrigued with the topic. The child doesn't simply memorize the tables, he also understands the mathematical concepts of multiplying, sees its relationship to dividing, and quickly learns short and long division. He not only absorbs the information but plays with it, moving beyond what the teacher requires. It's a thrill when you see your child grasping hold of subject matter in this fashion.

Get the backpack organized

Children are born with a brain capable of adapting successfully to a variety of settings: First the home, then preschool or child care, then the neighborhood, and later school.

You know your child can manage the school life if she knows the right time to raise her hand and ask the teacher a question or go to the principal's office for help. When your child organizes materials to complete a science project or history report and works as a team with classmates to finish a group assignment, she's doing well in the world of school. Keeping a backpack, desk, and notebook in reasonable order is another part of the process too.

If your child seeks out positive interactions with her peers, knows how to behave and follow the rules, she's well on her way to succeeding in this important environment called school.

Eaten up with curiosity

Let's say your child has held a strong interest in the weather and then, all on her own, becomes highly interested in the destructive effect of hurricanes or tsunamis. If the school curriculum matches your child's interest in this subject, school work then becomes part of the child's natural need to satisfy her curiosity. It's just great for your child when her natural curiosity meshes with a school subject. Or better yet, if hurricanes and tsunamis are not part of the fifth grade curriculum but your child's teacher picks up on your child's interest, the teacher might introduce the subject to the class or at least allow your child to study it and report on it independently.

Once children reach school age, their natural curiosity broadens to interests in current events, historical figures, scientific experiments, and mathematical equations. Some children find school curriculum an avenue for satisfying their expanding curiosity; others, sadly, do not.

Your child might be one who completes assignments as required but finds her real opportunities for learning outside of school. Since she does not find intellectual stimulation in the academic world, she learns on her own. She might do so through independent reading, an interest in computers, or extracurricular activities such as music, scouts, or sports. You probably hope that your child finds learning meaningful inside and outside of school but this occurrence is not always the case.

And if they don't want to learn?

It is most unfortunate when a child loses her natural curiosity and motivation to learn inside or outside of school. Some children fail to succeed academically because of attention deficit disorder, learning disabilities, family dysfunction, or troubles with drugs or alcohol. These stumbling blocks prevent some from actualizing their intellectual potential. If this is the case with your child, you may want to seek professional help, either inside or outside the school system.

Of course, you want your child to acquire academic discipline and to appropriately manage the world of school, but don't you also hope that your children will be learners for life? Think about how important it is that your children continue to develop their minds, to learn, to satisfy their curiosity, and to show interest in becoming successful in ever-broadening environments—including the world of work. If you don't see your child succeeding in school, do your best to help her follow her interests at home. You'll never regret it. When a child's mind is unused, it brings sadness to parent and child alike.

GeNTLe GuIdAnCe CaN hELp buIld chIldren's homEwork hAbIts

Wouldn't it be great if all kids automatically sat down to do their homework with no whining or complaints? But life is not usually like that. One of your kids may easily grasp homework responsibilities. Another may get distracted by the TV, extracurricular activities, or friends and siblings.

If your child comes home to an empty house or spends off-school hours at child care, homework might simply get lost in the shuffle and blur of these daily comings and goings.

If you really want your children to acquire personal discipline for homework, it's up to you to start early in the elementary years and to guide them to develop routines to complete homework assignments. Your role is tricky. Teachers make the assignment and it's a child's duty to complete them, but because they're completed at home, part of the responsibility lies with you.

"Home" is for "homework"

It's the parents' job to establish homework as a family value that takes high priority. It's an expectation that permeates the entire home atmosphere. To establish homework at the top of your family's to-do list, take on two tasks yourself:

1. See your role as your children's mentor to homework success.

2. Start shaping their homework behavior as soon as they enter school.

When your child comes home with that first assignment, sit down at the kitchen table and discuss with her what she needs to do. Don't view homework as a dreaded disease; instead, see it as an important rite of passage. "Homework! Wow! Your teacher sees you as mature and responsible enough to complete assignments at home. Good for you!"

At first, stay at the table with her, read your book, write a letter, pay bills, do your own homework from work. Your presence provides tacit control, keeping your child focused on the task at hand. Be interested in what your child is doing, but don't take over or do assignments for her.

As your child's mentor, you're available to offer assistance and guidance as needed. Make sure that when your child begins homework each evening, she's fed, rested, and relaxed, and the TV, telephone, and other distractions are eliminated from the vicinity. Do your best to set a regular time for homework that's as much a part of the family schedule as dinnertime, bath time, and story time.

If a child claims she has no homework, make it clear that she's still expected to work quietly on hobbies or read. As the weeks, months, and years go by, you slowly withdraw your presence as your child grasps homework responsibilities without you sitting right by her side or asking nightly what assignments she needs to complete. Stay interested in what your child is learning, but don't make your child's homework your responsibility.

Give homework help

At first it's okay to oversee your child's homework and help her by making baby steps toward excellence with specific suggestions like these:

• I see two incorrect problems on your arithmetic homework. Try these two again.

• Let's go over your spelling words one more time.

• You need to recopy your social studies homework. Although you've done well it's difficult to read.

With older kids, don't hesitate to show them how to outline a chapter from their science textbook. When studying for a math test, give a tip or two about checking work and doing the problems that are easiest first, saving the tougher ones for last.

Convey any study skills that worked for you, but then respect that your child may not follow your advice. Ultimately, each child must find his own way. Even if your son says, "Oh, Dad, you went to school in the old days, that's not the way we do it today," at least you've established your interest, clearly indicating you value academic responsibility and achievement.

Emotional meltdowns

When your child is emotional and upset, he can't complete homework assignments. Let him take a break, and allow him time for his emotions to settle. However, make it clear that he's still required to complete his assignments. While touching the child softly say, "You can cry and cry all you want, and I'm going to stay right beside you as long as you're upset. Then when you're finished crying, you'll need to complete your assignment." Taking this approach builds endurance for inevitable emotions that arise when academic challenges occur.

If, however, you sense that your child really isn't capable of completing the task, and that it's beyond his capabilities, set the assignment aside and call the teacher the next day.

The parents' role isn't to take over and complete their children's assignments, to harshly point out or correct mistakes, or to go on about how they could do better work. It's more effective to let children know they have all it takes to do the work and to tell them, "If you need help, I'm right here to assist you." A child may never ask for help but it helps to know that parents are nearby to lend a hand.

Four steps to success

As you set out to encourage your children to reach their academic potential, proceed cautiously. It's not effective to just tell your children to work harder, and you can't simply demand that your "C" student turn into an "A" student overnight. But you can set the stage so your "C" student can turn some of those Cs into Bs.

1. Keep the TV off between 7 and 8 P.M., or establish this rule: The house is quiet between 6 and 9 P.M. on school nights.

2. Involve your child in only one extracurricular activity. Do this especially if you notice that taking on more means that schoolwork suffers.

3. Forbid evenings out on school nights. It just doesn't work for most kids to play at a friend's house or go to the movies; they're too tired to do homework and then for school the next day.

4. Occasionally challenge your child with some kind of reward. "I see you got a C+ in math; I bet you can bring that up to a B. If you do, I'll give you $15."

When to stop pushing

Power struggles revolving around assistance with school work may erupt. Your child might resist your involvement, and her schoolwork could deteriorate. If this situation occurs, it's time to call the teacher, hire a tutor, or back off completely, allowing your child to come to terms with her academic responsibilities. If you drop out, do it in the following manner:

"You know that in our family schoolwork is important. You're smart, and you can do the work. I'm confident you'll figure it out on your own."

And when your child does well and receives a good grade, don't attribute it to luck or chance. Instead, say, "You got a B+ on your history test; good for you. Your grade reflects your hard work."

Rather than focusing only on grades, show genuine interest in what your child is learning and doing in school: "You're coloring a map of the United States. I'll show you the states I've been to; let's count them." Or for an older child, "I see that you're learning about the environment. What can we do as a family to protect the environment?" When kids go to school to learn, good grades follow. Your sincere interest supports acquiring knowledge.

Your Child may Not Excel In The Traditional Way

Are you involved in an academic tug-of-war with one of your kids? There are some kids who appear lazy, unmotivated, and just don't work up to their potential. These kids often are the ones who approach learning differently. At home they come across as intelligent and motivated, but in the traditional classroom, academic performance lags.

Your first step is to read Mel Levine's book the *Myth of Laziness*. From reading it you'll learn that your child's problem is often poor output. Such children can be talented in their ability to communicate verbally and can produce products relating to a beloved craft or hobby but stall when it comes to writing, penmanship, and spelling.

If you are blessed with this type of child, it's important to develop empathy and understanding for her. Such children may not succeed in the traditional classroom yet may end up being perfectly functional adults once they find their niche in the workplace.

It's vital to diagnose an academic deficit before the onslaught of puberty as becoming an adolescence often brings more complications.

A wide spectrum of dysfunctions exist that may be depriving a child of school success. It's daunting when a parent whose child appears perfectly typical in most areas of her life realizes that child is an innocent victim of the wiring inside the brain. Kids want to be productive; some just can't do it at school.

People are born with the drive to produce. Those who live and work with children who can't produce want to keep them from becoming casualties who believe that their work is worthless and perhaps always will be.

Such miswiring may show up in the child's memory, language, attention, motor function, and other processes required for mastery of school subjects. These kids often keep promising and intending to complete assignments but seldom come through. They often read far better then they can write; they can interpret information but somehow can't put what they learn to academic use.

If you suspect your child possesses some of the deficits described, first stop pressuring him. Lines such as: "Stay focused," "Get organized," "Practice spelling again," "Memorize those multiplication tables or else" and "Work on your penmanship more" aren't going to bring about positive change.

Second, talk with school personnel such as a teacher, learning specialist, or educational psychologist. Consider testing, tutoring, and a program tailored to your child's specific academic attributes and deficits. If a child is diagnosed with unique wiring, it's important to give that child the language for what she needs to work on academically. How can a person try to improve on something when she doesn't even know what it's called?

Third, talk up what your child does well and protect her from peers who may tease her because of poor penmanship or because the child can't complete math computations on the board in front of classmates. Offer the child the opportunity to recognize his strengths and weaknesses, and then teach her to rely on her strengths. Do your best to acquire an attitude that shows appreciation for your child's intellect and productivity, albeit separate from what she might produce in the classroom.

CHAPTER 8
FINAL THOUGHTS

So you think you know it all?

Just when you think you've got parenting licked, there are days and situations that simply take you aback. A family member dies, you're feeling sad and then all of a sudden you're struck with the realization that you must explain what's going on to your six-year-old. You wonder, "Will this unforeseen event rob my son of his childhood? Will he be able to bounce back from this adverse situation?"

Another day your ten-year-old may be disappointed that he didn't receive a birthday party invitation and then he's angry because you won't allow him to invite a friend to spend the night. Even though you know not to, you explain and then reexplain that you're having a dinner party that evening; nevertheless, his anger escalates. Although you know it's best not to, you blow up, too. Sometimes, no matter what, even the best, most informed parent loses her cool.

Knowing what to do when children cry, pout, stomp, and sulk because they're sad, disappointed, and angry or because they think it will get you to give in is an important skill to tuck in your back pocket and keep handy.

If you have a toddler, you'll observe that he doesn't play in a give-and-take manner with another child. In fact social engagements between toddlers are mostly about wrangling over toys or chasing one another around the room or park. During the preschool years friendships emerge as children play imaginatively together. Most older children are highly social, yet you're amazed when your child seems popular one day and friendless the next. What's that about?

The really bad days

Then the day arrives when you're in the car delivering your oldest child to soccer practice, the middle child to ballet, and the youngest to gymnastics. An hour later you're picking them all up, stopping for non-nutritious fast food on the way home, and skipping a family dinner once again. After your kids down their unhappy meals you yell at them to do their homework, which they work on halfheartedly in front of the TV. Although you know that exercise is important, suddenly you're struck with the possibility that maybe, just maybe, soccer, ballet, and gymnastics really aren't. After all, your kids are only ten, seven, and five years old. Why in the world are you doing most of your parenting behind the wheel of your car and from the sidelines?

But a laid back approach might be best

Can you make your child into a superstar on the athletic field? Should you try? Are athletes born or raised? It's tough to know your parenting role on the sidelines. It may be interesting to realize that if you really want your child to play basketball and you start him playing on teams at an early age, statistics reveal that the earlier you start a child in a sport, the younger he's likely to drop out of it. When should you start kids in organized sports and what's your role? It's another parenting dilemma to consider.

Then there's stress. If you're stressed out from your job, a relationship, or financial woes, your kids are, too. If you're a pushy parent or if your child simply can't manage the complexities of schoolwork, scouts, sports, and piano, children respond to all the stress in a variety of ways. Some sleep, others turn sick, a few resort to tantrums, and others retreat to their bedrooms. Stress harms your child's mental and physical health; it keeps their minds from developing. A little stress is okay, too much spells trouble. Each child can handle different amounts of it.

In the good old days Mom and Dad were a child's main influence. Sure there were friends, teachers, and religious influences, but today with the media—TV with hundreds of channels and the Internet with millions of web sites—you may begin to believe you don't have a voice or any influence. It's not so. Your children look to you for ideas, information, and your perspective; don't deny them your influence.

Raising tough cookies

Childhood is sacred. No parent intentionally wishes his child thrust into the big, bad world to manage unpleasant situations. Nevertheless, a car may strike your child's pet or his best friend might move to Cincinnati.

Some parents divorce, siblings are born, grandparents turn sick. Even if by some miracle you could protect your child from first hand adversity, the media is often the culprit in robbing children of their childhood. News, movies, and TV programs expose children to far more than what's likely to happen in your comfort zone.

How do kids cope? The resilient child, the one who bounces back when faced with adversity, manages better than others. Some children are born resilient, while others can acquire resilient characteristics.

Even though your natural parenting instinct might be to soften a blow to your children by managing a difficult situation for them, it might be more important that you cultivate attributes of resiliency. Then your children won't, from fragile character, permanently retreat, display needy behavior, cease to mature along their developmental timeline, or become depressed when misfortune strikes.

Build emotional strength. When your child responds to an unsettling situation with fear, anger, disappointment, or sadness, don't try to talk him out of what he's feeling. Instead, identify his emotion, and convey understanding and empathy. Whatever you do, don't send your emotional child to his bedroom. You need to stay with him until his emotions settle down.

Resilient kids aren't stoical; when faced with adversity, they respond emotionally, recoil temporarily, and then, more often than not, return to their prior emotional state.

Build problem-solving skills. Once emotions subside, it's time to engage your child's brain. Identify the problem at hand, and ask your child what he can do to solve the problem. Validate the child's ideas, offer a few suggestions yourself, but don't dominate. Encourage your child to use his own resources to manage the situation even if his solution is somewhat immature.

From the preschool years on, resilient children display an interest in solving problems rather than giving up or depending on others to manage situations for them. They're task and solution oriented.

Develop an internal locus of control. When your child faces hardship, resist victimizing him with a "poor you" approach. Instead, validate the difficulty of the situation but exude confidence that he can figure out a way to manage the situation effectively.

Resilient children believe in their own effectiveness. Although external events may have caused their problem, they assume responsibility for a solution. They don't consider themselves victims.

Elicit support from others. When troubles arise, encourage your child to ask for help from a teacher, coach, clergy, friend, community support person, or expert. Then take this attribute one step further, and prompt your child to help others.

The naturally resilient child has the uncanny knack of finding a nurturing person in or outside the family to support him through troubled times. It's a magical combination of independence coupled with an ability to ask for help when needed. By late elementary school the resilient child does what he can to help others in the family, neighborhood, or community when they're experiencing distress or discomfort.

Support your child's hobbies. Hobbies are not a frivolous pastime. They're a source of pride that your child can call on when part of his world seems to be falling apart. Your job is to show interest and help your child to cultivate the hobby on his terms.

When the resilient child faces turmoil, he turns to a hobby or a special interest for solace. It might be cooking, computer games, or a baseball card collection that brings the world back into focus. In addition, the activity builds competency and provides a source of pride.

Offer an optimistic view of life. Your influence is most effective here. When problems arise, recognize them but point out any silver lining in the troubled cloud. Help your child see that in time things will get better and life will again offer many moments of happiness.

Resiliency goes along with a faith that things will work out as well as can be reasonably expected, and negative events can be surmounted, thus giving meaning to life and a reason for commitment and caring.

Encourage communication. Learn to listen to your children and encourage them to express their feelings and opinions. Invite them to describe troubling situations.

The resilient child effectively communicates problems and feelings, thus gaining positive attention, backing, and ideas from interested friends, family, and adults.

Promote academic and intellectual excellence. Do all you can to help your child use his intellect in and out of school.

The resilient child is not necessarily intellectually gifted, but each uses his talents optimally, working to reach his potential. If a child is intelligent and scholastically competent, these attributes are positively associated with the ability to overcome great odds.

More than anything else, when a difficult situation occurs, in order for children to bounce back, it's essential they connect with at least one healthy adult in or outside the family. If you're that person, your task is to help the child believe that he has everything necessary to be successful and overcome adversity.

Matthew—an example of a resilient child

Consider ten-year-old Matthew, who one day received the news that his beloved grandfather who lived next door had died from a heart attack. Not only were Grandpa and Matt buddies, but Grandpa was also Matt's after-school caregiver. Given the sad news, Matthew retreated immediately in tears to his bedroom. Dad followed, and they cried together until Matthew fell asleep. While Matthew continued to be sad and obviously missed his grandfather, he also took action to manage the situation. He asked his father many questions about death and why his grandfather died.

The next day and days following, Matthew located and displayed pictures of Grandpa, talked with friends about their deceased grandparents, asked for a few mementos of Grandpa, and even participated in his funeral. Then with support from his parents, he started to solve the problem of who would now care for him after school. Matt displayed resilient behavior.

THE TRICKY WORLD OF EMOTIONS

If you're in the middle of helping your child with homework, and your child turns on the tears, your job is to attend to the tears first before insisting your child finish his homework.

If you've told your child to put away the blocks and your child stomps about in an angry manner, you've got to focus on the emotions of the moment before requiring your child to complete the task. In parenting, children's emotional responses are a wild card, they override all else that's occurring at that moment.

When a child responds with emotion, it's critical that you convey sincere understanding. Do so by putting his emotional response into words: "You're angry; you wish you didn't have homework. This assignment seems difficult," or "You're really angry that I've told you to put the blocks away. You wish they could remain on the living room floor forever."

This approach serves two purposes. First, that the child realizes that you understand his point of view, which communicates love and builds intimacy between you and your son. Second, he hears the words that are appropriate in such situations. Eventually, rather than wail, he'll express himself civilly with words.

Your emotions v. their emotions

When your child shifts into high gear with emotion, shift yourself into low gear and move toward your child. Stay by his side for five minutes or so. Say to the child: "You can be as angry as you like, I'm not going to allow you to hit me or destroy property, but you can be angry. I'm going to stay right here with you as long as you're angry, and when you're finished being angry, then you'll need to complete your homework assignment."

"You can be upset that it's time to put the blocks away. I'll stay with you as long as you're angry; and when your anger goes away, then you'll need to put the blocks in the box." If your child continues to carry on, gently escort him to his room, put his teddy bear in his arms, and tell him, "You need to tell your teddy how mad you are. He wants to know."

Telling a child to stop feeling angry, sad, disappointed, or frustrated although well-intended, only exacerbates the emotions of the moment. Meeting a child's intense response with a parent's demand to stop emoting usually serves no purpose. He'll only get more emotional and have a harder time learning to manage his emotions.

If possible, notice and talk about emotions when they first begin to well up. By doing so, you can sidestep an eruption, smoothing out the child's emotions before he becomes enraged or totally distraught.

Ride it out

Resist offering an explanation, using reason, or offering a rational thought when a child is out-of-control with emotion. No one can think very well when emotional. It's best to wait until the child calms down. Then, later, when the child is calm, explain the situation rationally. His ears will be open to your insights.

If you try to talk a child out of his ideas, he'll only carry on further, trying to convince you his perspective is legitimate. By validating the child's opinion and emotional response, they magically disappear.

Don't worry; you won't be raising a child who wears his emotions on his sleeve, always needing you to unruffle his emotional feathers. In time, your child is able to nurture himself through emotional situations. He'll know emotions surface and he'll know how to manage his emotions all on his own. Children gain this skill somewhere between eight and twelve and then lose it again through the emotional roller coaster ride of adolescence.

HOW yOU CAN hELP yOUR kIdS mAkE fRIENDs

It's likely you hope your children develop lasting friendships. It's unlikely that you're aware that children learn about friendship from you. It's true. The children who are the most competent in social situations have parents who are nurturing. This fact doesn't mean that you are your child's best friend, but it does mean that most of the time you want to come across in a friendly manner.

Before waging a zealous friendship campaign to make sure your youngster is competent in social situations, go back to the Nurturing Parents Check List (see page 10–16). Check out once more your skills as a nurturing parent.

Ask yourself:
- ❏ Am I affectionate and friendly when interacting with my child?
- ❏ Do I consider my child's feelings, desires, and needs?
- ❏ Am I interested in my child's daily activities?
- ❏ Do I respect my child's point of view?
- ❏ Do I express pride in each of my children's accomplishments?
- ❏ Do I offer support and encouragement during times of stress?

If you rank high as a nurturing parent you're likely to see the same nurturing behavior you exhibit toward your children reenacted between your children and their peers. From parent to child these qualities equate to nurturing; from child-to-child, they're exhibited in friendly interactions.

Some children just naturally acquire many friends, others only a few; and some children buddy up with one best friend at a time. Regardless of your child's number of friends, it's important for parents to do what they can to support those friendships:

A few pointers
- Make your home welcoming to friends.
- Encourage your child to join a group—scouts, sports, hobby, religious—and then support it with your time and interest.
- Don't embarrass or ridicule your child in front of peers.
- Avoid labeling your child as shy, mean, or friendless. Such labels solidify the tendency, preventing the child from changing into a friendly person.
- Don't saddle kids with too many responsibilities and schedules. Friendships take time to develop in relaxed and somewhat unstructured situations. When the child is little it's called "play"; when the child is older it's "hanging out."
- Allow your child to buy that pair of jeans everyone is wearing. Superficial forms of conformity signify group acceptance and participation.

Toddlers either play by themselves or with another child. When both children have a train engine to scoot along the track, they're enjoying a social experience toddler style, even though it's not interactive.

Preschoolers seek out playmates and even play cooperatively. "I'll build the house, you build the garage." "No, I want to build a barn." "Okay, we're building a farm." If, however, a third child enters the scene, she'll most likely be excluded. It's beyond most preschooler's mental and social ability to play cooperatively with more than one child at a time. The adage "two's company, three's a crowd" pertains perfectly to children under seven years old.

By age eight, children can relate in social situations to more than one child at a time. Their relationships become egalitarian and reciprocal as kids gradually work to acquire the rules and skills of friendship. It's a natural maturation process that's refined when kids have many opportunities to play, compete, problem-solve and work together.

During the school years, you'll see glimpses of positive and mature relationships involving kindness, thoughtfulness, caring, and sharing, but these qualities don't fully take hold until high school.

There will be times when you'll witness or hear of disconcerting interactions that go on between kids. As most know, children sometimes can be downright nasty.

"She cheats. She can't play." An isolated incident of frankness toward one who cheats, whines or brags often helps the offender remedy her ways.

Merciless teasing and taunting is different. "She wears glasses. She's a nerd, a geek, a dweeb." When such incidents are repeated by the tormentor and unprovoked by the victim, that's bullying, and it should not be tolerated by teachers, parents, or youthful bystanders.

Most children, from time to time, face problems with peers. When this happens to your child, listen to his feelings, and when the tears subside, offer small bits of advice. This approach provides the child with the strength to face those same kids at school the next day.

Rejection from friends and rejection at home is too much for any child to bear. During troubled friendship times, your child needs acceptance and understanding; he needs you to be his friend.

When it comes to learning the hard knocks of friendship, experience is often the best teacher. If kids come up with solutions to their problems and don't depend on their parents or teachers to step in, it's usually best.

Most kids eventually learn fairness, social justice, and how to get along. The key ingredients are time and practice, along with parents and teachers standing by as ultimate protector.

Funneling the friendship factor

If you want your children to be well liked, guide them to:

• Not be demanding in social situations. Demanding kids who whine or pout and then grab all the cookies will have trouble making and keeping friends.

• Take turns when engaged in conversation, playing games, or involved in activities or classroom interactions. Coach your children not to dominate or interrupt. You probably remember a kid in school who insisted on being first, talked too much, and interrupted others. It just wasn't fun to be around that kid. Those children are the ones who don't receive many invitations to birthday parties.

• Respond promptly when someone speaks. No one likes to be ignored. By responding to your child, he'll learn to respond to others. That's what friends do for one another.

• Follow the logic of a conversation; help your child to stay focused on a conversation and to not get off track.

Children who display competence in these four areas are well-liked by their peers. If your child has trouble in these areas, your role is to exude patience and understanding. These skills come easily to some children; for others, they seem to be simply more difficult to master.

HaVe YoU gOnE iNtO hObBy OvErDrIvE?

One day you're likely to wake up and ask yourself, "Exactly when am I supposed to enroll my child in extracurricular activities?" and you'll wonder, "How many are appropriate?" On the one hand, you won't want to let the opportunity slip by of sending your child down the path to becoming an Olympic athlete—cultivating from a young age your child's interest or innate talent. On the other hand, you don't want to unnecessarily stress your child or yourself by hauling your kid to numerous scheduled activities, making everyone cranky and on edge.

The voice of reality tells you that your children most likely will not earn their living from sports or music careers. Nevertheless you'd like to promote some lifelong interests that will provide many enjoyable hours away from the demands of academia and career.

With the right balance and the right motives, extracurricular activities can be rewarding for both you and your child. There are, however, many questions and practicalities that you need to consider.

Good reasons, bad reasons

Once your child turns two years old, you'll wonder if now is the time to begin music class, ballet, or gymnastics. Enrolling your child in ballet is so tempting. You just know your toddler will look so darn cute in a tutu. Then when kindergarten begins you'll most likely feel pressure from your parenting peers, who are buying soccer shoes and a piano in order for their child to join a team and begin lessons. Before you follow the parenting crowd, ask yourself why you're doing it.

Good: simple, stress-free fun

If going to music class or gymnastics is an enjoyable, hassle-free experience for you and your preschool child, do it. If the activity is a time to enjoy your child away from the demands of your home or work life, do it. If you live in a neighborhood isolated from families with young children, and a class could supply the opportunity for your child to interact with peers and a place for you to meet other parents, do it.

Bad: getting a head start

If you're signing your child up for one enrichment activity after another because you believe an early start will secure a lifelong interest or give your child the competitive edge in high school sports or music, think again. If you start a child in extracurricular activities too early—before his body is developed to perform the skills required, before his mind is able to understand the strategy of a game or a musical concept, before his emotions can manage the pressure of competition and performance, or before he acquires the social skills to understand sportsmanship and the discipline of practice—you're likely to turn him off to the activity instead of providing the benefits you might wish.

Bad: pushing for a prodigy

Parents hear of music and sports prodigies whose parents recognized their child's innate talent and then supported the talents without hesitation. If you discover you've got a prodigy on your hands, you'll have some difficult decisions to make about nurturing your child's amazing innate talent. But prodigies are few and far between. Most likely your child will develop talents and interests alongside his peers in the standard developmental time line.

Good: positive peer groups

Keep in mind that in addition to the learning skills connected with a sport or musical instrument, extracurricular activities offer a hidden benefit: Your child is usually surrounded by a positive peer group. As children grow up, they naturally move away from your influence and attach themselves to peers. With certainty you'd rather your child's friends spring from ballet class rather than an interest in hanging out at the mall or watching talk shows and MTV.

Practical considerations

What does your child like to do? Notice your child's interests and the interests of his peers at ages seven and eight. Give your child a choice of activities. It could be soccer, Girl Scouts or Boy Scouts, piano, swim team, or music lessons. If it's soccer he chooses, realize you can't just drop your child off at the soccer field; you need to be there to cheer him on, support the team, notice and talk up his best efforts.

How many activities can kids manage? Each child is different. Some can manage two activities, others more. If you've got three kids, each in two activities, watch it. Although your children may thrive on the enrichment of the activities, you, on the other hand, may stress yourself out. With the pressure of going in so many directions, you may resort to yelling at one to suit himself up for practice and snapping at another to grab her piano books and climb in the car for a lesson. You might better maintain family harmony by limiting each child to one activity.

How will you juggle everything? If you're all going in so many different directions, what happens to family meals? When does homework get done? Do these important daily events play second fiddle to ballet or guitar lessons? Parents need to decide what they value most, and what's most important in the long-term for their children.

Complaints and quitting

Let's say your son enthusiastically chooses soccer. You purchase the shoes and uniform. He starts practice, even plays the first game, but now he resists each afternoon when it's time to go to practice. He complains and wants to relax by playing and watching a little TV. You're tired of the complaints; you feel like you're dragging him to the soccer field. Yet once there, you see he's enjoying her teammates and the sport.

Why the resistance? Many children don't move easily from one activity to another. So, when he complains, express a little understanding: "I know you'd like to stay home and relax." Then set the limit: "Nevertheless, you have a duty to your team. It's time to climb in the car; we'll be off in five minutes."

When should you let kids quit? This is the basic rule for your parenting thumb: If the child goes into an activity with a frown but comes out with a smile, keep going. If your child is like six-year-old Erica, who started out enthusiastic for ballet but ended up hiding out in the hall through the lesson, it's time to call it quits, or better yet, offer that she take a break from ballet with the option to try again when she's older.

Alternatives

At-home options. Let's say you want your child exposed to music so you enroll yourself and your toddler in a music activity class, two 30-minute sessions a week. Your toddler seems to enjoy the sessions, but going is stressing you out. Instead of hauling your tot to the class, you decide to provide a musical experience right at home, and on your own schedule. You invest in maracas, bells, a drum, and toddler musical recordings. This is an excellent alternative for both you and your child. You might even invite a neighbor and her child or your brother and his youngster to join you.

Unique pursuits Each of your children may have unique interests that need nurturing. Resist pushing a younger child to follow in his siblings footsteps. Alan, for example, never wanted to be in organized team sports like his brother or to take piano like his sister.

At age seven, much to his family's delight, he developed an interest in baking, developing a specialty in making cookies.

Then at age ten, he ran for office in student government. By this time his parents had all but given up hope of him pursuing sports when, lo and behold, he signed himself up for skiing, an individual sport in which he immediately excelled.

Playtime Kids, just like adults, need downtime—it's called play. Play is a necessary ingredient to healthy development. If your child is overscheduled with activities, he'll miss the opportunity to engage in the emotional, social, intellectual, and physical benefits of unstructured and child-guided playtimes.

Hobbies Many older children find satisfaction from pursuing a hobby, like playing chess or collecting baseball cards or stamps. Hobbies are intellectual pursuits, but they're also stress reducers because they're directed and managed by the child.

Overscheduling

Notice what your children do when nothing's scheduled. Do they wander off to entertain themselves with a game, hobby, or project or are they bored and restless? Do they immediately turn to video games, TV, or the Internet? One result of too many scheduled activities is that some children don't know how to manage themselves when there's nothing planned. And some, overly stimulated from going from one event to the next, have trouble concentrating or sleeping.

If you understand the dangers of starting kids too young and overscheduling them but you have sane, sound reasons to sign your children up for extracurriculars, by all means do so.

Sports

If you sign your youngster up for a team sport, keep in mind that kids who excel are generally the ones whose body type fits with the sport (tall for basketball, short for gymnastics, long and lean for swimming) coupled with innate talent. It's important for you to be realistic. Don't expect that your tall, pudgy daughter is likely to excel in gymnastics.

Once you've acquired realistic expectations for your child's ability to perform on the playfield, then you need to look to your own demeanor on and off the sidelines. While you can't change your child's body or increase his natural ability, how you approach this experience will have a lot of influence on your child's success or failure and on her willingness to continue or drop out.

The days when children roamed the neighborhood with their pals on bicycles, climbed trees, and played baseball in vacant lots, having fun and getting exercise are over for many children for a variety of reasons. You're likely to susbstitute extracurricular activities and make them a priority. It's just as important to know when such scheduled activities are not in your child's or your best interest, thereby calling it quits or pursuing an alternative activity or agreeing that downtime is just fine and even beneficial.

Here are some dos and don'ts:

✗ Don't attach love to winning or performing. Communicate to your child that while you're excited when he hits a homerun or scores a goal, you love him just the same no matter how he performs or if his team wins or loses.

✗ Don't scream at your child from the sidelines. On the field your child is trying to pay attention to the ball, his teammates, and his coach. If you're yelling directives at your child, he's likely to lose concentration and flub up. Plus you're likely to embarrass him. Always keep in mind that you're a cheerleader offering thumbs ups, high fives, claps, and a few whoops and hollers.

✗ Don't get in a confrontation with the coach. If there's a problem with coaching, the time to discuss the situation is not during the game and the place is not on the sidelines. You serve yourself and your child best by giving a phone call after the game when your emotions have died down to discuss a coaching issue.

✗ Don't impose professional standards on peewee sports. They're kids, not paid professionals. Children's bodies and minds are in the process of mastering the skills and strategies of the game they're playing. If you're overly demanding with unrealistic expectations, it's likely your child will give up and drop out, not reaching his athletic potential.

✓ Do support this activity. This includes taking your child to practices, playing and practicing in the backyard, and standing on the sidelines on cold wet Saturday mornings cheering your child and his team on. If you want your child committed to the sport, you need to be committed, too. Additionally, you act as a buffer for your child as you explain the ups and down of team play and competition.

✓ Do withdraw your child if coaching is out of line. Some coaches, while well meaning, don't have the training to work effectively with young children. Some are overly harsh and demanding. If you see your child not thriving under the tutelage of a coach, allow your child to drop out until next year. It's your call.

✓ Do prepare yourself to be the parent of a bench warmer. How will you handle this? Even though all kids are supposed to have equal time on the field or court, some children will play more than others. Yours may be the one sitting out much of the game. It's your job to be dignified in your role as the proud parent of a bench warmer.

✓ Do notice what your child does best. Talk up that one caught ball, or that one walk to first base. It's so easy to point out and dwell on the errors of your child's on-the-field ways. Doing so will harm your child's self-esteem and work against him reaching his athletic potential. Make your goal a 5–to–1 ratio—five compliments to one criticism.

✓ Do take your child for a physical. Some young bodies will not be ready to handle rigorous throwing and running. You don't want your child's body to wear out before it's fully grown. Don't be so zealous about your child's sport's life that somehow his body is permanently harmed from overuse on the playing field.

real life parenting

Giving team sports the "OK"

Karin signed up each of her boys, beginning at age five, for soccer. Why? To provide them with a positive peer group, good exercise, and simple fun. Karin's reasons for hauling her boys to soccer practice and cheering them from the sidelines are valid. Making such an extra-curricular activity a priority was legitimate and beneficial for Karin's family, and it can be for yours as well.

WaTcH eAcH cHiLd's sTrEsS qUoTiEnT

Many children, like their parents, face stressful moments every day. A parent, however, might scoff at the mention of her child being stressed out. Most would say it is parents—not children—who are stressed. It's not only the rigors and responsibilities of raising children but managing the home and dealing with challenges in their personal and work lives that boosts parents' stress levels.

Parents do have these stress factors. For now, however let's set those stress facts aside and notice stress in the lives of children. First of all, it's important to realize that when parents are under stress, children are, too. Additionally, children feel stressed from such seemingly mundane events as fighting with a brother or sister, not knowing what to do next, going to bed early, and being expected to eat food they do not like. And then there are more obvious events such as starting child care or school, or the death of a grandparent that pile on stress for children.

For many children there are even more taxing events: Parents separating, living in a blended family, and both parents working outside the home. On top of these stressors, children feel stressed when watching violence on TV, being over-scheduled with homework and extracurricular activities, and being pressured to perform or behave beyond their age and ability.

When kids are bombarded with such stressful events, their mental and physical health are negatively affected. What could be worse? The child's body becomes vulnerable to illness, and learning, thinking, and remembering are jeopardized.

This must be emphasized. When children are under stress they are more likely to be sick, and their ability to think, learn, and remember is impaired. Every parent wants her child to be healthy. Plus, every parent wants her child to use his mind not only in school but also in all sorts of situations. Stress negatively effects a child's intellectual development.

Also, no parent wants her child to get hooked on stress. The long- and short-term effects are too harmful to the mind and body. Instead, parents need to stress-proof their child. If you start when your child is young, this stress-proofing can last a lifetime.

Step 1 to stress-proofing

Knowing how much stress is enough and how much is too much for each child.

Stress-proofing children is a better approach than attempting to take all stress away. As children take on new challenges, whether in their personal lives with families and friends or intellectually and academically at school, stress occurs—and it's not all bad, it's even necessary. In order to learn and manage new environments, children need to experience a certain amount of stress. Each child has a different stress quotient; it's your job to calculate what that is for each of your children.

Step 2 to stress-proofing

Working into your everyday routine activities that relax and calm your child.

Such stress reducing activities are simple to learn and execute, plus they do wonders to release stress for both parent and child. These activities are as simple as breathing deeply, singing a peaceful song while driving in the car, imagining a quiet forest while the child holds her favorite blanket or teddy bear, or jumping up and down on a mattress placed on the garage or basement floor.

In time, when these stress-reducing activities become habitual, the child can call on them himself without you. There are many benefits. The child thinks and behaves better. He is better able to soothe himself when stressed, handle frustration and anger, control negative reactions in a conflict, think and remember, and cooperate with others.

A child who can calm himself is able to control impulsive behaviors. He's more likely to notice feelings and respond in thoughtful ways. An unstressed child learns to plan ahead and make positive choices, solve problems and feel empathy for others.

Step 3 to stress-proofing
Knowing when to slow down, not take on any new activities, or call it quits.

It's tempting to keep your children busy, taking on one more activity or attempting one more challenge. But all of a sudden you might become perfectly aware that doing so is not going to benefit your child. It's tough to slam on the brakes when everyone else seems to be zooming ahead at full throttle. Sometimes you—the responsible parent—need to call a halt when you see that your child isn't sleeping, is frequently sick, or is emotionally falling apart.

Stress isn't going away for parents or children, so both need to find ways to relax when stressful moments occur. Stress reducing strategies contribute to a physically, emotionally, and intellectually healthy approach to family life.

Kids of All aGes tAkE tHeIr CuEs FrOm PaReNtS

There's an interesting phenomenon that occurs when a child approaches twelve months old. When your active little crawler or walker approaches a new or unusual object or toy, he will look over at you before getting too close. If the child could speak, he'd say, "Tell me about this unusual thing that I discovered in the living room. What's your opinion? Should I approach it or not?"

If it's an electrical outlet at a neighbor's house (of course, you've already child-proofed your outlets), you'll look in horror, shake your head, and move toward the child to make sure he doesn't touch it. If it's a vacuum cleaner, you might approach it with the child to show him how it works. If it's a new toy, you might smile, nod, and gesture that it's OK for your child to have it.

When you and your toddler are walking along the sidewalk, he might eye a cat. Your child might start toward it but then glance at you to see if touching the animal is a good or a bad idea. If you're at the grocery store with your preschooler and a person you don't know greets him, he will look to Mom or Dad to see how to respond. Parents should offer coaching.

Parents are their children's social reference, not only when they're little, but also as they grow up and take on new and more complex social situations and challenges. Starting at age one, children are on the go and highly curious, two qualities that could get them into trouble. Humans are programmed to survive, and children somehow know they can't do so alone. Therefore, they look to the most powerful people who have helped them survive so far.

This job of being a child's social reference comes naturally to most parents. In potentially dangerous situations, they keep their children no farther away than they would their purse, briefcase, or briefcase.

As children get older, parents tell them about the world around them, offer their opinion, and provide explanations. With words, body language, and facial expressions, parents give children clear and consistent messages about what's OK and not OK.

Once children start school and branch out into the world beyond Mom and Dad, they begin to refer to others for social guidance: Peers, teachers, grandparents, and popular culture. Nevertheless, parents still remain powerful references. Children need to know where parents stand.

How do you feel about lying, stealing, cheating, violence, premarital sex, alcohol, drugs, gun control, politics, and religion? Tell your children.

Teenagers may roll their eyes when you offer information, but so be it. Muster up the courage and let them know where you stand anyway. They'll think through your ideas and use them in class, on the ball field, and even at parties.

Parents are home base, peers are at first, the media and popular culture are on second, and other adults play third. Children always come back to home plate—particularly when called out at first, second, or third base—until they, as adults, establish themselves as their own home plate.

InDeX

AcKnOwLeDgMeNtS

Thanks to all who provided insights, stories, inspiration and support:
Debbie Englund, Jan and John Reed, Linda and Andrew Starkenberg, Alison
Gopnik, Andrew Meltzoff and Patricia Kuhl, Kathy and Monti McBeth, Sandi
Wright, Shirley Eubanks, Elizabeth and Lisi Hall, Erica Englund, Karen, Blake and
Hanna Warmenhoven, Regen Dennis, Sue Anderson, Alexis and Troy Phillips,
Lacey, Mike, and Jamie Franz, Shannon and Greer Smith, Julie, Darryl, Collin, and
Andrew Peeples, The Dike Family, Victoria Tennant, Janelle and Christopher
Raney, Terrill Chang, Gwen Raney, and many students from parenting classes and
readers of my columns in *The Seattle Times*, lhj (*Ladies Home Journal*).com, and
bh&g (*Better Homes & Gardens*).com.